CW00430538

HEINEMANN
SCHOOL
MANAGEMENT

Improving School Attendance

by
Susan Hallam

Heinemann Educational
A division of Heinemann Publishers (Oxford) Ltd,
Halley Court, Jordan Hill, Oxford OX2 8EJ

OXFORD   FLORENCE
MADRID   ATHENS   PRAGUE
MELBOURNE   CHICAGO   AUCKLAND   SINGAPORE
TOKYO   IBADAN   NAIROBI   MEXICO   KAMPALA   GABORONE
PORTSMOUTH NH (USA)   SAO PAULO   JOHANNESBURG

© Susan Hallam 1996

99 98 97 96
10 9 8 7 6 5 4 3 2 1

A catalogue record for this book is available from the British Library

ISBN 0-435-80048-5

Typeset by TechType, Abingdon, Oxon.
Printed and bound in Great Britain by Clays Ltd, St. Ives plc.

Contents

Contents

Contents

Contents

Introduction

This book aims to help teachers, school governors and those acting in managerial capacities in schools to understand why pupils do not attend school. Based on this understanding, it aims to develop a range of strategies to improve attendance.

The ideas and approaches described in the book are based on a nationwide survey of good practice funded by the Calouste Gulbenkian Foundation. The ideas have all been tried by schools and found to be successful. The reasons pupils do not attend school are many and complex. Because of this, there are no 'quick fix' solutions. The differing nature of each school community means that what is successful in one school may not be successful in another. For this reason a range of approaches are suggested which can be developed to meet the needs of your school.

The book is divided into six sections. Staff development needs are considered in relation to each section as necessary.

Section I: Getting started

Chapter 1 examines the complex nature of non-attendance, taking into account the roles of the pupil, the parents and the school. Chapter 2 outlines national patterns of attendance and draws attention to those times when children are at particular risk of slipping into habits of absenteeism. Chapter 3 describes ways in which schools can establish their own levels and patterns of attendance, providing a baseline from which improvement can be measured. Chapter 4 proposes ways of raising awareness regarding attendance and generating ideas for change.

Section II: Setting up policies and procedures

Chapter 5 gives a detailed account of the ways in which schools can improve the day-to-day management of attendance. Chapter 6 addresses the question of writing and communicating policy and

1

Chapter 7 introduces ways by which, over time, the school can evaluate the policies and procedures that it has adopted, and make changes based on progress, feedback and experience.

Section III: Factors within school affecting attendance

Chapter 8 tackles the question of anxiety caused by school, leading to illness. Chapter 9 examines how a school's ethos, procedures and practices may unintentionally deter some pupils from attending and outlines some of the attractions outside school which may tempt pupils away. Chapter 10 considers what can be done to make school more attractive to pupils taking account of the physical, social and learning environments of the school. Real case studies demonstrate the diversity and complexity of absence.

Section IV: Factors outside school affecting attendance

This section examines the roles of family, community and society in promoting and hindering attendance and suggests ways that schools can develop partnerships with homes and communities to reduce absenteeism.

Section V: Ways of working with absentees

Chapter 14 considers procedures for dealing with persistent absentees, the legal position and ways of facilitating pupils' return to school. Chapter 15 introduces recent group work which has been successful with those at risk of experiencing attendance problems and those who are already disaffected.

Section VI: Useful information

This section includes a brief resume of the DFEE guidelines on attendance, and further sources of reading, help and information.

▇▇ Why attendance matters

Underlying the purpose of this book is an assumption that regular attendance at school is important for the well being and future prospects of children. The negative effects of poor school attendance are also felt by schools, teachers, parents, communities and society as a whole.

Pupils

Today, young people need to achieve higher educational levels than ever before. Absence, for any reason, has a negative effect on learning. Non-attenders, therefore, jeopardise their future opportunities. Progress at school can also lead to a sense of achievement and growing self-confidence. Persistent absence prevents this. Non-attenders are also at risk in the community and vulnerable to the temptation of alcohol, drugs and crime.

Schools

Levels of pupil attendance have recently become of even greater importance for schools. Examination results and figures for authorised and unauthorised absence are now published in the press and scrutinised by the public. If pupils do not attend school regularly their performance in public examinations will suffer. Schools have a particular interest, not only in encouraging pupils to attend, but also in maximising learning and achievement while they are there. Attendance levels and a school's policies and practices in monitoring, maintaining and improving them are considered in OFSTED inspections.

Recent attempts to engender competition between schools have also increased the pressure to create a good impression within the local community. Groups of pupils seen out of school, during school hours, may tarnish positive impressions of a school. Concern about attendance also demonstrates the level of care that a school has in relation to its pupils and is a sensitive indicator of morale in pupils and staff.

Teachers

The effective planning and management of pupils' work becomes impossible when attendance is erratic. Frequent absence creates additional work in helping pupils to catch up, while also taking time away from other pupils.

Parents

Prosecution may occur if children do not attend school regularly. This can occur even when parents wish a child to attend but are unable to persuade him or her to go. Persistent non-attendance at school can also be an indicator of problems which the child is experiencing outside school.

Local communities and society at large

Non-attendance can lead to an increase in some types of crime and put some people in the community at risk. At a national level it represents a waste of educational resources, potential skills and knowledge, and consumes the valuable time of police and social workers.

It is therefore in the interests of pupils, parents, teachers, schools and the wider community to encourage full attendance at school.

SECTION I
GETTING
STARTED

1 Old problems – new solutions

Truancy is not new. Since education became compulsory children have skipped school. By the early 1900s, 88 per cent of children under 12 were registered at school, but, on average, only 72 per cent attended on a daily basis. Attendance was affected by poverty, the need to work, domestic responsibilities, apathy, inclement weather, attractions outside school and the value attached to education by pupils and parents.[1] Almost 100 years later, the picture has changed very little.

▇▇▇ Terminology

Historically, the term truancy has tended to be used for all unauthorised absence from school. Numerous regional expressions have also developed, e.g. mitching, skiving, bunking off, dodging, wagging, sagging, dolling, slamming, bobbing and cutting. Today, when pupils are described as truants, stereotypical images are invoked. Truancy tends to be equated in people's minds with delinquency. This is an oversimplification.

Some have confined the term truancy to those cases where pupils have made a conscious decision not to attend school. But such decisions may be made when pupils feel their help is essential at home to look after someone who is ill, or because they are afraid to attend school. Given the negative connotations associated with the term truancy, its use in these cases is hardly appropriate.

Even where pupils have no obvious, morally valid reason for non-attendance and the label truant seems applicable, closer examination of the circumstances may reveal a more complex picture. For instance, the pupil may be finding the work beyond their capabilities, so that school becomes a place where they are constantly confronted by failure. Or, they may live in an area of high unemployment, where job prospects

7

are negligible even for the well qualified. In these circumstances school may be viewed as a waste of time and the need for self-esteem, and respect from peers, may be sought through other activities.

Because of the complexity of reasons for non-attendance and the negative connotations associated with the word truancy, its use in this book will be restricted to those occasions when it is referred to by others. The terms non-attendance and absence will be used instead.

Who is to blame for absenteeism?

The causes of non-attendance at school have been variously laid at the door of parents, schools, communities and pupils. It is now generally accepted that the causes are complex and multi-faceted. It is the way that members of these groups relate to each other that is important.

The role of parents and the school

Prior to the introduction of compulsory education, parents were regarded as crucially influential in school attendance.[1] Many kept their children away from school to supplement the family income, the earnings of children preserving many working class families from destitution. Sometimes, children were required to help look after younger siblings. In other cases parents were actively hostile to education or simply apathetic about ensuring that unwilling children went to school. This lack of parental enthusiasm was justified to some extent by the poor quality of educational provision. But as schools became better, teachers more efficient and instruction produced satisfactory results, attendance improved. Some parents even kept their children at school, in the face of financial difficulties, if this enhanced future job prospects.

Much has changed since the late nineteenth century. Children are now legally required to have an education, which, for most, means attendance at school. The inter-relationships between the attitudes of parents and educational provision are therefore less transparent. Nevertheless, many of the factors outlined above are as important today as they were then. The table below illustrates a recent attempt to chart the interplay between the official and unofficial attitudes of schools and parents to attendance.[3]

These categorisations draw attention to the possibility that schools and teachers may officially disapprove of absence but yet unofficially condone it. For instance, where a pupil is disruptive in class, teachers,

Categories of absence from school

Officially induced	Absences forced on pupils by schools, e.g. closures, shortages of teachers, disciplinary action, exclusion
Officially approved	Absences officially recognised as being attributable to personal or family reasons, e.g. illness, bereavement, religious observance
Officially illicit but unofficially condoned	Absence which is officially illicit but which tends to be ignored by teachers and Education Welfare Officers, e.g. absence of disruptive pupils, pupils staying at home to complete coursework for GCSE
Officially illicit but parentally approved	Absences instigated by parents, e.g. getting a child to help at home or undertake paid work
Officially illicit but parentally condoned	Absences which parents do not approve, but where they feel unable or unwilling to enforce attendance
Officially illicit and parentally disapproved	Absences where officials and parents disapprove
Internal and illicit	Absence from lessons, even though the pupil is in school

Derived from Carlen, Gleeson and Wardlaugh (1992), *Truancy: The Politics of Compulsory Schooling*, Open University Press.

understandably, may be relieved that the pupil is absent so that they and the remaining pupils, can work undisturbed. The absence is then likely to go unreported, with minimal, or no, action taken to improve the pupil's attendance. Similarly, if a pupil is missing school to complete coursework for examinations, this is likely to be condoned.

Parents may also hold contradictory attitudes to school attendance. In some cases parents may clearly wish their child to help at home or in the family business and actively encourage absence. In others, they may officially disapprove but in fact, by their actions or lack of action, condone the absence. For instance, if their own experiences of school have been negative, they may perceive, and refer to, school as a waste of time. Such attitudes will inevitably affect their child's perception of school and the importance they attach to attendance. More subtly, when a child is absent from school parents may express pleasure at their being at home, even though publicly, they support the child's attendance.

Community and societal factors

In the late nineteenth century, with increasing competition from abroad, employers, particularly in manufacturing industries, began to realise the importance of education. Similarly in the late twentieth century, leading figures in society have suggested that improvement in educational attainment is a national imperative for economic success. Nevertheless society transmits conflicting messages to young people. Pupils are exhorted to attend school to obtain qualifications to prepare them for employment, while high levels of unemployment mean that some may never have regular full-time work. Similarly, pupils who are expected to behave responsibly towards others may be penalised when they miss school to take care of others, even when no other care provision is made. Society appears to have dual standards. Officially, non-attendance at school is condemned but many factors which make it difficult for some to attend are left unchanged.

The nature of the pupil

It has also been suggested that the characteristics of individual pupils are responsible for non-attendance. Persistent absentees have been categorised as maladjusted, and various personality and behavioural characteristics have been ascribed to them. This approach has been of limited use in improving attendance. However, a consideration of motivational perspectives[3] has proved useful in counselling. This has identified four types of unauthorised absentee, whose behaviour can be viewed in relation to two motives, one internal, anxiety – sensation seeking; the other social, conformity – negativism.

Anxiety or sensation seeking is related to the pupils' internal level of arousal. Some pupils find school over-arousing. They experience this as anxiety. Absenteeism is a way of reducing anxiety. Other pupils find school under-arousing, experiencing boredom. These pupils actively seek excitement and sensation and may skip school to find it.

Conformity or negativism relates to the pupils' desire to conform to the wishes of others or to rebel. Conforming pupils may skip or attend school to comply with the wishes of friends, parents or teachers. The pupil who adopts a negative approach is rejecting pressure to conform and rebels.

Considering pupils' unconscious motives in this way can aid our understanding of their motivation. However, schools should not neglect motives which are rational and conscious. If aspects of school are particularly unpleasant or children have other concerns, which they feel need to take priority, e.g. uncompleted coursework, caring for younger siblings, then they may take a rational, conscious decision that it is better to stay at home and not go to school.

▓ All non-attendance can be harmful

Since the days of compulsory education, 100 per cent attendance at school has never been achieved. Some of the reasons for this may be perceived as legitimate, for instance, illness; others may be considered illegitimate, for instance, missing school to watch TV, help in the family business. Whatever the causes of non-attendance, the extent to which it occurs will determine its effects.

Many of us may recall skipping the odd lesson and retrospectively thinking that it was not particularly harmful. One body of thought has even gone so far as to suggest that pupils who never miss school are lacking in initiative. So at what point does skipping school become harmful? The response to this question depends on why we think children should go to school. Do we believe that schools are places where children are prepared for making their own valuable, personal contribution to society? Or are they institutions where learning has a narrower focus related to employment? Or are they places where pupils are merely 'kept off the streets'? The view taken in this book is that schools should be places where children are helped to grow into responsible adults, who feel valued by society, and in turn wish, and are able, to make a valuable contribution to that society.

If we take this perspective, any absence from school should give cause for concern either because:

- the child is ill, experiencing problems at home, experiencing difficulties at school;

or

- the child is behaving irresponsibly.

Viewed in this way any absence becomes an indicator of distress or alienation, which should trigger immediate action.

▓ The crucial role of the school

While the responsibility for school attendance should be shared between children, their parents, schools, communities and society at large, schools are in the best position to take the lead in instigating action. They have a crucial role to play in developing new solutions to problems which have changed little over the past hundred years.

New solutions

This book offers practical advice on how to tackle attendance issues in your school. The information is based on a nationwide survey of good practice. The approaches that are suggested have all been tried and found to be successful in some schools. Because the reasons for non-attendance at school are complex and depend on individual and community factors it is not possible to provide a simple recipe for success. Success depends largely on the commitment of staff, pupils, parents and the local community. For this reason each school needs to establish those practices which are acceptable to, and work for, their staff, pupils and parents. The aim should be to make everyone want to be at school.

What you can achieve

By selecting from, working through and implementing those ideas presented in this book which are relevant to your school, you can expect to:

- Raise awareness of the importance of attendance at school;
- Improve attendance across the school;
- Improve the attendance of persistent absentees;
- Create a more positive school climate.

Improvements of this kind require effort and take time. The processes of monitoring, raising awareness and generating ideas for change may take an academic year or longer. If this is undertaken carefully and with the full support of staff, pupils, parents and the community there **may** be immediate effects. With continued effort these can be sustained over time.

One hundred per cent attendance will not be achieved by all pupils all of the time. Pupils will always have legitimate reasons for absence and from time to time particular circumstances in the lives of some pupils may mean that the habit of attendance is broken. Speedy action on the part of the school can make a real difference in preventing this from becoming a persistent problem.

▧ What you will need

Factors important for success include:

- A commitment to improve attendance as part of the school development plan;
- Commitment from the headteacher and the governing body;
- A core group of staff to co-ordinate, monitor and evaluate progress;
- Support of the whole school staff;
- Time in meetings of governors and staff to discuss attendance issues;
- Time to enable pupils to be involved in the planning and implementation of strategies;
- The involvement of parents;
- The support of outside agencies, particularly the Education Welfare Service.

The remaining chapters in this section enable you to make a start in the task of improving attendance in your school.

---

1 Old problems – New solutions

Summary

Truancy and its causes are not new.

In our technological age, high levels of achievement in education are of crucial importance to:

- pupils
- parents
- schools
- communities
- society

The responsibility for ensuring that children attend school regularly should be shared between these parties.

Schools must take the lead in developing solutions to the problem of non-attendance.

To facilitate change schools require:

- Improving attendance to be part of the school development plan
- Commitment from the headteacher, staff and governors
- Support from parents, the local community, outside agencies
- Persistence and long-term commitment to change

2 National trends

Obtaining accurate information

It is extremely difficult to obtain **accurate** and **detailed** information regarding absence from school at a national level.

- Overall attendance

  This can be assessed by reference to school registers. Schools are required to make this information available for publication.

  Comparisons of percentage attendance between schools are problematic as individual patterns of absence are obscured. For instance, two schools may both have an 89 per cent average attendance rate. One may have high average attendance from the majority of pupils, with a small number of persistent absentees reducing the overall rate. The other may have a fairly consistent absence rate across the whole school. Percentage attendance figures reveal very little of the actual pattern of attendance in any one school.

- Authorised and unauthorised absence

  When reporting absence, schools use different criteria to distinguish between authorised and unauthorised absence, even when operating within the statutory legal framework and the DFEE guidelines. Schools may also vary in the level of vigilance they apply in establishing the authenticity of absence notes and the legitimacy of explanations. This makes it difficult to assess accurately the incidence of unauthorised absence in schools. It also makes meaningful comparison between schools impossible.

- Numbers of persistent absentees

  The current method of presenting the figures for unauthorised absence does not distinguish how often each individual child has been absent, making it impossible to ascertain persistent absenteeism at a national level.

■ Absence from individual lessons

Overall registration figures do not take account of pupils missing lessons after they have registered. Nationally, skipping lessons after registration is usually assessed by means of questionnaires to pupils. How reliable they are is open to question. Pupils may find it expedient to minimise their absenteeism if they feel that the survey may not be totally confidential. But, if they are guaranteed anonymity from officialdom they may exaggerate to impress peers. As such surveys are invariably undertaken during school time, information is not collected from pupils who are absent. This is likely to include some persistent absentees. This means that there is likely to be an underestimation of the level of absenteeism.

■ Estimates from other sources – EWOs and parents

Parents, as they risk prosecution if their children do not attend school regularly, are unlikely to be a reliable source. EWOs have been inconsistent in their definition of what constitutes persistent absenteeism. This makes comparison across studies impossible.

■ Time of survey

The timing of a survey also affects the outcome. For instance, attendance is generally lower in the Summer term. There are also regional variations. In official surveys, the period of the survey may vary from a day, a week, a term or a school year.

What we know about current levels of absence from school

Despite these problems of measurement it is possible to outline some trends.

Overall attendance nationally

National figures for overall attendance rates vary from 83 per cent to 92 per cent depending on the particular survey used.

The official figures for attendance at schools in England in 1993–4 as published by the DFEE show an overall 94 per cent attendance rate in primary schools and 91 per cent in secondary school.

■■■■ National authorised absence figures

The national figures for authorised absence for different kinds of secondary schools are shown below. These compare with an overall average for secondary schools of 8.1 per cent. In special schools the authorised absence rate is 8 per cent, in City Technology Colleges (CTCs), 6.7 per cent and in independent schools, 3.2 per cent. The bar charts represent the percentage of half days missed.

Authorised absence by type of school in England 1993/4

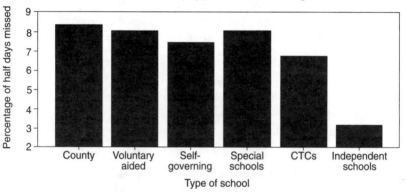

Derived from the National Pupils Absence tables 1994 DFEE

■■■■ National unauthorised absence figures

The national average for unauthorised absence in maintained secondary schools is 0.9 per cent. The graph illustrates the differences between types of school. In special schools the percentage rises to 2.4 per cent, in CTCs it is 0.4 per cent and in independent schools the figure is less than 0.05 per cent.

Unauthorised absence by type of school in England 1993/4

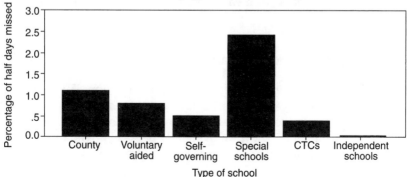

Derived from the National Pupil Absence Tables 1994 DFEE

These figures represent averages across year groups. They do not take account of differences in absenteeism as pupils progress through school or differences between classes.

▆▆▆▆ Surveys of pupil-reported absence

Some surveys have attempted to take account of post-registration absenteeism and have based their assessment on pupils' responses to questionnaires. The largest of these[4], commissioned by the Department for Education, was conducted in 1992 and concentrated on pupils in years 10 and 11. The percentages of pupils reporting 'blanket truancy' (missing a whole day) or 'post-registration truancy' are given in the diagram below.

Pupil reported post-registration and blanket truancy in years 10 and 11, 1991–92

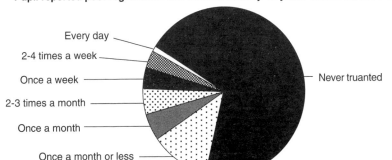

Derived from *Truancy in English Secondary Schools: A report for the DFEE* by the Truancy Research Project 1991–92, HMSO: London.

Of those reporting absenteeism, 64 per cent claimed that they were involved in 'blanket truancy' and 'post-registration truancy'. 25 per cent of year 11 pupils reported missing lessons without leaving the building.

On the days when the survey was undertaken 17 per cent of pupils were absent from school. The figures are therefore likely to be an underestimation. Poor levels of attendance in years 10 and 11 have been confirmed in other studies.[5,6]

Although less attention has been given to pupils lower down the school, there is some evidence that even in year 7 as many as 8 per cent may play truant sometimes or often.[5]

▆▆▆▆ Differences between areas and schools

There are considerable differences in absenteeism between geographical areas and individual schools within these areas. A survey of 40,000 young people which concentrated on attendance in year 11[6] focused on three kinds of unauthorised absence: serious absence (missing several days a week), selective absence (missing odd lessons and single days) and occasional absence (missing the occasional lesson). The diagram below illustrates the overall national figures. 6 per cent of young people reported serious unauthorised absence and 10 per cent reported selective absence. Contrary to popular belief no difference was found between males and females.

Truancy among year 11 pupils: self-reported from 40,000 Youth Cohort respondents Youth Cohort Study 1984–8

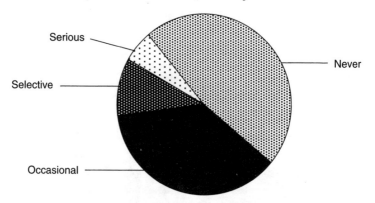

Derived from Gray & Jesson, 1990, *Truancy in Secondary Schools amongst Fifth-year Pupils,* Sheffield University

Truancy among year 11 pupils in the inner city: self-reported from inner city Youth Cohort respondents Youth Cohort Study 1984–8

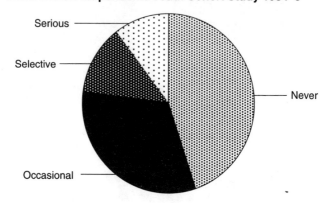

Derived from Gray & Jesson, 1990, *Truancy in Secondary Schools amongst Fifth-year Pupils,* Sheffield University

What the survey did reveal was that overall more unauthorised absence was reported in inner city areas. A comparison of the two pie charts reveals the differences. In the inner cities, 10 per cent of students reported serious truancy, while 13 per cent reported selective truancy.

Differences between schools

The students in the survey attended over 2,300 secondary schools around the country. In the great majority of schools (over 70 per cent) the proportion of serious truants was low, although a few persistent absentees were to be found in most schools. In 20 per cent of secondary schools, 10 per cent of pupils in year 11 reported serious absenteeism. In approximately 8 per cent of schools serious absenteeism was reported by more than 20 per cent of year 11 pupils. When absenteeism is at this level, the staff and the local community clearly face a major problem.

Schools who fell into this category were not only inner-city schools, although the incidence of inner-city schools facing such problems was almost twice the level of other schools. This is illustrated below.

Levels of serious truancy in inner-city schools and schools elsewhere

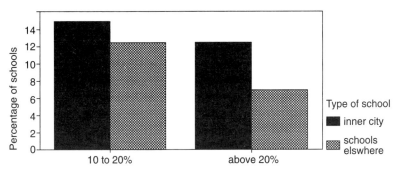

Percentage of pupils reporting serious truancy

Derived from Gray & Jesson, 1990, *Truancy in Secondary Schools amongst Fifth-year Pupils*, Sheffield University

It is clear that while inner-city schools have more difficult problems, some inner-city schools tackle them more effectively than others.

General trends

Despite the problems in obtaining accurate measurements of unauthorised absence from school a number of trends have been observed:

- There is usually an increase in absenteeism as pupils transfer from one phase to another, e.g. primary to secondary, middle to upper;
- Children with significantly higher than average absence at one school are likely to continue to be poor attenders at the next;
- There is a general increase in absenteeism as pupils progress through secondary school with the highest level of unauthorised absenteeism in year 11;
- In all phases girls are absent more than boys, although there is little difference in their rates of unauthorised absence;
- There are changes in absenteeism during the school year. Different surveys show different patterns. It is likely that each school has its own particular pattern;
- Half-term holidays, INSET days and other breaks in routine can precipitate increases in absenteeism;
- Absenteeism is greater in inner-city areas;
- Even within the same catchment area schools have different levels of attendance. Schools can and do make a difference.

---

2 National trends

Summary

The national average for authorised absence is about 8 per cent.

The national average for unauthorised absence is just under 1 per cent.

Some general trends in attendance can be observed. Absenteeism:

- increases as pupils progress through school;
- increases when pupils change school;
- increases when there are interruptions to routine;
- is not consistent through the school year;
- is higher in the inner cities.

Even within the same catchment area schools have differing attendance levels.

Schools can and do make a difference

3 Establishing the pattern of attendance in your school

The initial phase of a plan to improve attendance has three stages:

- identifying the existing patterns of attendance in the school;
- raising awareness;
- generating ideas for change.

You need to start with an understanding of the current pattern of attendance. With this information your school will be in a strong position to take effective action.

Schools are already required to present some of this information to the Department for Education and Employment and for OFSTED inspections. The monitoring process also:

- raises awareness of particular problems among staff, pupils, parents;
- establishes a baseline against which to measure success.

What do you need to collect?

The simplest solution is to focus on overall attendance. This removes uncertainty regarding the classification of absence as authorised or unauthorised. In institutions of all kinds levels of attendance are now accepted as useful indicators of morale and can be adopted by schools as one measure of their success in creating a positive school ethos.

To establish a thorough profile of the school's attendance pattern the following information is required:

- the baseline attendance rates for classes, year groups and the whole school;
- identification of the particular types of absenteeism prevalent in the school;

- particular lessons where attendance is poor;
- pupils or groups of pupils whose absence gives cause for concern.

It is important to ensure that the information is accurate and that there is consistency across the school in the way that it is collected.

How can the information be obtained and collated?

First, a group of staff who are committed to improving attendance need to be given responsibility for collating and reporting on the attendance profile of the school. The membership of the group should reflect the management structure of the school and include staff with responsibilities for attendance issues at all levels. The group may also include office staff, Education Welfare Officers, etc.

School registers

School registers can provide information regarding authorised and unauthorised absence. This can be broken down to give detailed information regarding year groups, classes, gender, ethnic groupings or other groupings which the school feels may be relevant to understanding its attendance pattern.

In addition to considering patterns of attendance in pupil groups the school should also consider patterns in time, e.g. days of the week, months, terms, before or after holidays or staff training days, and in different years. This can help in identifying times when absenteeism is more likely and taking preventive action.

Finally, the patterns of attendance of individuals can be considered. This may draw attention to pupils whose overall attendance level is broadly acceptable, but where the pattern is erratic. It may also enable the identification of pupils in years 7 and 8 who appear to be at risk of becoming persistent non-attenders in years 9, 10 and 11.

This information can be collated more easily if the school has a computerised registration system. However, with staff cooperation it is possible to collect perfectly adequate information without computerised systems.

Collaboration with local feeder primary schools in monitoring attendance patterns of individuals can be useful in the identification of 'at risk' pupils.

▨ Lesson attendance

Attendance at lessons can be monitored either by keeping registers for each lesson or by undertaking a survey of pupils' reports of non-attendance.

Many schools already keep records of attendance for each lesson, but these are not always checked against school registers. This means that pupils can miss individual lessons undetected. During the monitoring procedure comparisons needs to be made to assess the extent of non-attendance after registration.

An alternative approach is to use questionnaires. These also provide a means of finding out why pupils do not attend particular lessons. They will not be as reliable in assessing lesson attendance as teacher-kept records because:

- pupils may not remember accurately how often they have skipped school

- they may choose to distort the information, from a sense of bravado or fear of being found out.

Developing a questionnaire is discussed in the next section.

▨ Presenting the information

Once the information has been collated it will need to be compiled in a form which is easily understood. Presentation in visual form, using bar charts or graphs is very effective. Figures might also be presented in tables. Some examples are given below.

The graph demonstrates clearly the improvement in overall attendance in 1993/94 when the school adopted measures to improve attendance. It also shows how the pattern of attendance changes over the school year.

Once the patterns of attendance in your school have been identified, attention can be turned to finding out the reasons for non-attendance.

A computer printout in table form for years 9, 10 and 11, giving details of attendance for Autumn and Spring terms and authorised and unauthorised absence

Year registration	Total attendances	Total authorised absences	Total unauthorised absences	Total students	Total students with absences	Total students with unauthorised absences	% students attending	% unauthorised absences	% students with unauthorised absences
11F	5533	740	309	28	25	22	84.06	4.69	78.57
11G	4800	523	533	24	23	22	81.97	9.10	91.67
11J	4919	545	131	23	22	16	87.92	2.34	69.57
11M	4428	865	544	24	22	21	75.86	9.32	87.50
11R	5166	995	719	29	27	28	75.09	10.45	96.55
11W	5036	513	549	25	25	15	82.58	9.00	60.00
11	29882	4181	2785	153	144	124	81.10	7.56	81.05
10A	6383	575	141	30	29	18	89.91	1.99	60.00
10B	6385	665	247	31	29	19	87.50	3.38	61.29
10D	5706	968	666	31	29	27	77.74	9.07	87.10
10G	6193	685	181	29	28	22	87.73	2.56	75.86
10M	6034	771	287	31	29	12	85.08	4.05	38.71
10P	6470	417	320	31	25	25	89.77	4.44	80.65
10X	0	264	0	3	3	0	0.00	0.00	0.00
10	37171	4345	1842	186	172	123	85.73	4.25	66.13
9G	6143	789	217	31	29	21	85.93	3.04	67.74
9H	5187	411	35	25	23	11	92.08	0.62	44.00
9J	6059	510	139	28	26	20	90.32	2.07	71.43
9M	6192	719	164	29	28	16	87.52	2.32	55.17
9S	6101	531	140	29	27	22	90.09	2.07	75.86
9T	6034	844	196	29	28	17	85.30	2.77	58.62
9X	740	63	17	6	6	4	90.24	2.07	66.67
9Y	5883	671	100	28	28	11	88.41	1.50	39.29
9	423399	4538	1008	205	195	122	88.42	2.11	59.51

Comparison of weekly attendance for years 7-11 for 1992/93 and 1993/94

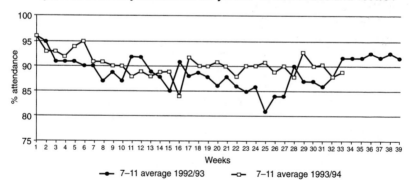

Weeks

—●— 7–11 average 1992/93   —□— 7–11 average 1993/94

■ Establishing the reasons for absence

There are a number of ways that the reasons for absence can be established. All involve consultation with others.

Pupils are the most reliable source of information about why they do not attend school. This is particularly so if the information is collected anonymously, or in such a way that they do not need to admit to skipping schools themselves.

Pupils' views can be tapped through: discussion, for example, in tutorial groups; by the use of questionnaires; or by undertaking individual interviews. This latter strategy is likely to be most effective with persistent absentees, where they have nothing to fear from the interview.

▬ Pupil discussion groups

Tutor groups or personal and social education classes can be used as vehicles for raising issues relating to attendance at school. Rather than asking direct questions relating to personal non-attendance, which some pupils may find threatening, tutors can focus the discussion more generally. Some possible starting points are outlined below:

Why do we have schools?
Why do you come to school?
Do all children attend school every day?
Why do you think that some don't attend?
Do some pupils skip particular lessons?
Why do you think that they do that?

A number of issues may be raised through such discussions:

- general reasons why pupils do not attend school;
- particular lessons that are disliked;
- particular teachers who are disliked;
- difficulties with friends at school;
- difficulties at home.

Discussions of this nature can pose problems for the teachers who are involved. For instance, if colleagues are criticised by pupils, how are they to deal with this? If a decision is taken to instigate such discussions, guidelines need to devised which are acceptable to all staff. Despite such possible difficulties, the information obtained can be invaluable in highlighting problems pupils may have with aspects of school or home life.

Discussions relating to attendance at school can also lead to a consideration of the importance of education and in themselves be valuable in persuading pupils that attending school is 'a good idea'.

An alternative to discussions is to devise a questionnaire to be given to all pupils.

Pupil questionnaires

A survey by questionnaire can establish the level of non-attendance in the school and the reasons for it.

Set up a coordinating group to be responsible for devising and administering the questionnaire and analysing the findings. Prior agreement will need to be reached with staff regarding the nature of the material to be collected.

There are a number of important factors to bear in mind. These are outlined below:

- ensure that any information you require about class, age, year group, gender, etc. is asked for clearly;
- ensure that the information remains confidential;
- ensure that the instructions are clear, e.g. whether to tick one box, several boxes, circle responses, write answers;
- use colloquial language;
- provide examples if necessary;
- make questions concrete and specific;
- avoid double negatives;
- allow opportunities for open-ended comment.

Senior pupils can be involved in the development and administration of the questionnaire. This can be a useful way of raising their awareness and ensuring their commitment.

When devising the questionnaire, it is important to identify clearly the information that you wish to collect, for instance:

- how often pupils skip half days of school;
- the reasons they give for this;
- how often pupils miss individual lessons;
- which lessons they miss;
- why they miss particular lessons;
- what they do when they are not attending;
- how they feel about school in general.

A sample questionnaire, which you may copy for use in your school, is given below. Many of the questions require open responses. This allows students to express their views spontaneously, without prompting. If you prefer, you can insert a list of reasons suggesting why they may not attend school and insert boxes for them to tick.

Sample questionnaire

We are asking you to fill in this form because we want to know what you really do and think. Do not put your name on the form. None of the teachers will know what you have written. It will be completely confidential.

Please **ring** one of the following responses

What school year are you in?

7   8   9   10   11

What gender are you?

Male   female

Please ring the category that best describes you:

Bangladeshi	Black African	Black Caribbean
Black other	Chinese	Indian
Pakistani	White	Other

1. In the last half term have you ever stayed away from school, all day, when you were not supposed to?

   Yes   No

   If you answered yes, how often did you do this?

   2–4 times a week   once a week

   2–3 times a month   once a month less often

   less often

   Why did you stay away?

   _____

   _____

   _____

   _____

   _____

2. In the last half term have you ever registered for school and then left?

   Yes   No

   If you answered yes, how often did you do this?

   2–4 times a week   once a week

   2–3 times a month   once a month

   less often

   Why did you do this?

   _____

   _____

   _____

   _____

3. If you answered yes to the questions above, what did you do during the time when you should have been at school?

_____

_____

_____

_____

_____

4. If you answered yes to the questions above, what would encourage you to attend school more regularly?

_____

_____

_____

_____

_____

5. In the last half term, have you ever skipped individual lessons?
   Yes   No

   If you answered yes, how often did you do this?

   2–4 times a week   once a week
   2–3 times a month   once a month
                  less often

6. Please list the lessons that you skipped and give your reasons.

   Lessons   Reasons

   _____

   _____

   _____

   _____

   _____

7. If you answered yes to the questions above, what did you do during the time when you should have been in lessons?

   _____

   _____

   _____

   _____

   _____

8. If you answered yes to the questions above, what would encourage you to attend those lessons more regularly?

   _____

   _____

   _____

   _____

9. What do you most like about school?

_____

_____

_____

_____

_____

10. What do you most dislike about school?

_____

_____

_____

_____

_____

Thank you for your time filling in this questionnaire.

When undertaking the survey make sure that the questionnaires are completed in a calm atmosphere and that the children are assured of complete confidentiality. If necessary make arrangements for staff other than form tutors to administer the questionnaire. If children are likely to have difficulty reading the questionnaire, provide staff to go through the questions with them. If pupils have problems writing their responses, someone, perhaps another pupil, may help them to fill in the form.

If children are absent when the questionnaire is given out, make sure that they are provided with one on their return. This is particularly important in relation to non-attendance issues, as those absent from school are likely to include those whose responses are most important.

If the survey is to be repeated as part of an ongoing evaluation of progress, ensure that it is undertaken at the same time each year. As we saw in Chapter 2, the time of the school year has an effect on levels of attendance.

Interviews with pupils

Interviews can be undertaken with all pupils, but this is an extremely lengthy and time-consuming process. However, individual interviews with pupils who are known to have poor or erratic attendance records can be very useful, providing detailed information about their reasons for non-attendance. Interviews are more flexible than questionnaires and enable relevant issues to be explored in greater depth. They can also be useful for children who have literacy problems.

Interviews need to be conducted by someone who the pupil feels they can trust. Confidentiality needs to be assured. Nevertheless, there is a danger that pupils will not be honest. Even pupils already identified as poor attenders may have reasons for disguising the causes of their absenteeism. For instance, they may be afraid that revealing problems at home may lead to the break up of their family.

To ensure that the information can be compared with that from other interviews it can be useful to devise a form on which to collect and report the findings. This need not be complicated. It may provide spaces for information regarding year group, gender, ethnic grouping, academic progress, behaviour difficulties, family background, referrals to outside agencies and the main issues arising from the interview. Section V of the book provides a detailed account of the ways that one might collate information regarding persistent non-attenders.

Teacher groups

Once detailed information is available regarding patterns of attendance, teacher groups can be set up to discuss possible reasons for the patterns. While this may not yield such accurate information regarding the reasons for non-attendance as that obtained directly from pupils, teachers may find it less threatening.

Discussions might begin by focusing on a number of issues:

- the problems created for the school by poor attendance;
- the problems created for teachers when pupil attendance is not consistent;
- how teachers feel when pupils do not attend their lessons;
- the reasons why pupils might not attend. The example case studies given in Sections III and IV of the book might be used to stimulate discussion;
- the reasons why particular curriculum subjects may be unpopular (data collected from your own school or the figures provided in Section III could be used as examples).

Meetings with other professionals

Those working in or with the school from outside agencies may have valuable information as to why pupils do not attend. Particularly important in this respect are Education Welfare Officers (EWOs), who have a broad knowledge regarding non-attendance in general and also have information relating specifically to your school. EWOs could be consulted individually by a member of the team dealing with attendance or might contribute to more general discussions with groups of staff.

Where school counsellors are employed, they too can provide valuable information regarding the problems which pupils are experiencing in and out of school.

Educational psychologists, social workers, health care workers and police working in the community might also be consulted.

Parents and community groups

Parents can also be consulted regarding attendance issues. As parents are legally responsible for ensuring that their children attend school, it is often assumed that they know when their child is absent. In fact, parents often have no means of knowing whether their child has been to school or not. It is the school's responsibility to ensure that parents are aware of poor or irregular attendance.

In some circumstances parents may be aware that their child is reluctant to attend school but be unaware of the specific reasons. This is particularly likely where the child has physical symptoms because of anxiety (see Chapter 8). Children, even when pressed, are often reluctant to tell their parents about their problems at school, for instance if they are being bullied, or are afraid of particular teachers. Sometimes, parents may be aware of difficulties but be afraid or unsure about how to raise them. Schools have much to gain from providing opportunities for parents to raise such issues. Meetings can be set up to focus specifically on attendance. These might be of a general nature to explore parents' views or may be related to individual pupils. Where communication is made by letter, tear-off slips can be provided to encourage parents to respond.

3 Establishing the pattern of attendance in your school

Summary

For half-day attendance use school registers to establish:

- days, weeks, terms, etc. when non-attendance is high;
- groups and individual pupils who exhibit particular patterns of non-attendance.

To assess non-attendance at lessons:

- take lesson registers over a period of time;
- check lesson attendance against school registers and half-day attendance;
- carry out a survey of pupils.

To establish the reasons for absence:

- set up pupil discussion groups;
- carry out a survey of all pupils;
- interview known poor or erratic attenders;
- set up teachers' discussion groups;
- seek information from EWOs, educational psychologists, school counsellors, or others who may have relevant knowledge;
- seek information from parents.

4 Raising awareness and generating ideas for change

Having established the level and nature of the attendance problems in your school, the next stage is to raise awareness and generate ideas for change. Changes may be required concerning the everyday management of attendance; specific attendance problems; or more fundamental whole-school issues.

Methods of raising awareness

For sustained improvement, the impetus for change must come from everyone concerned. Staff, pupils, parents and the local community need to be persuaded that it is a good idea for pupils to attend school. Messages about the importance of attendance need to be communicated to all these groups. These messages must be easily understood and remembered.

Theatre in education groups provide an excellent resource for raising issues regarding school attendance with pupils. They can also be invaluable in addressing other areas of potential difficulty, for example, bullying, racial harassment, drug abuse, interpersonal relationships. Assemblies can also focus on attendance, with invited speakers, e.g. a representative from the Education Welfare Service, introducing key issues. Poster, song writing or drama competitions can foster interest and provide visual and aural reminders to maintain awareness over time.

To provide information to pupils, staff and visitors, an attendance noticeboard can be set up in a prominent position in the school foyer. This will need to be regularly updated with current attendance information, which might include figures for the whole school, year groups, or classes, depending on the policy adopted. It can also display posters which draw attention to the advantages of attending school regularly and the dangers of staying away.

Social events, e.g. carnivals, open days, fetes, school plays and concerts, can be utilised to spread the message within the wider school community. The press can be invited to provide publicity, while local companies may be willing to provide prizes to reward good attendance. Local firms can also be approached with a view to providing work placements for persistent absentees, dependent on good attendance at school.

Communication can be made more effective with the use of humour, visual material, and the translation of material into the first languages of the school community. You could use:

- cartoons;
- videos;
- songs;
- leaflets;
- posters.

The performing and creative arts departments in school can be of great value in generating ideas and putting them into practice.

Ways of generating ideas for change

Staff commitment is vital for success. To promote this, every attempt must be made to involve staff in the process of generating ideas for change and the subsequent decisions about which ideas should be implemented. Ways in which this process may be undertaken are indicated below, beginning with administration, then specific attendance issues, finally considering whole-school change.

Improving procedures for recording, monitoring and following up absence

The monitoring procedure may reveal aspects of everyday procedures relating to attendance which require improvement. These are best resolved by those undertaking the duties on a daily basis. This may include ancillary workers, form tutors, heads of year, those involved in pastoral care and those from agencies outside the school, e.g. EWOs. When the monitoring of lesson attendance is considered input from subject teachers will also be required.

Designed for Clapton School, Hackney

Chapter 5 outlines systems of recording, monitoring and following up absence, which have been demonstrated to work effectively in schools around the country. These may be helpful in providing ideas to generate discussion. There is no simple formula for success, each school needs to develop systems which are suited to its particular needs, taking account of the staff involved and the characteristics of the school community. For instance, there is little point installing complex, expensive computer systems if they will not be used effectively, or expecting parents to telephone the school when their children are ill, if most of them do not have easy access to a telephone.

Problems to generate discussion

1. Discussion in tutor groups has revealed that a large proportion of poor attenders have difficulties with the curriculum because of poor basic skills. They often find lessons boring because they cannot cope with the material. This leads them to skip lessons. What can be done?

2. A number of pupils have been identified who are working relatively long hours, in supermarkets, video shops, restaurants, doing milk rounds. There has been a gradual decline in their performance at school and their attendance has become erratic. What should you do?

3. Your school is on two sites. Students and teachers have to travel between the two. There is a constant problem with late arrival for lessons and some pupils do not turn up at all. What can you do?

4. Teacher groups discussing attendance issues have raised the problem of pupils missing lessons, perhaps for legitimate reasons, and then finding it difficult to catch up with ongoing work. In some cases, this has become such a serious problem that it has led to further non-attendance. What can teachers do?

5. A work experience period was arranged for the penultimate week of term. In the week following it attendance in that year group fell. What should the school do?

6. A questionnaire to students, addressing issues relating to attendance, showed a disproportionate number of pupils skipping language lessons. The pupils reported that they did not like learning foreign languages. It was 'a waste of time'. What could be done to change this situation?

7. A questionnaire revealed that some pupils were afraid of coming to school because of bullying by older pupils. This was a particular problem at breaktimes, and on the way to and from school. What should the school do?

■ Tackling specific problems

The monitoring procedure may have revealed specific aspects of school practice, e.g. relating to particular groups of children, subjects, particular teachers, timetabling, uniform, which are acting to deter pupils from attending school. If specific difficulties of this nature are identified, solutions need to be developed by task groups, made up of those directly affected. This may include the pupils themselves. The activities undertaken to generate ideas for change will depend on the nature of the problem being tackled.

Focused discussion may assist in providing solutions to some problems. This needs to centre around the difficulties highlighted during the monitoring process. The box opposite outlines problems which have been raised in some schools. These may not be applicable in your school.

Other difficulties may require more open-ended discussions. In these cases brainstorming is a useful technique. First, as many ideas as possible are generated and listed, with no criticism allowed. After the initial brainstorm the ideas can then be considered for their practicality. The kind of problems which particularly benefit from brainstorming are those which are broad and open ended. Some examples are given below.

Examples of tasks which may require brainstorming

1. How can we persuade those parents who normally have no contact with school to become more interested in their children's education and school activities?

2. How can we improve links with local primary schools?

3. How can we encourage pupils to be punctual?

4. How can we influence the ways that pupils at the school behave when they are
not actually in school?

5. What can we do to raise pupils' expectations regarding their academic work?

6. How can we improve pupil motivation?

Whole-school issues

The methods described above are equally appropriate to generate ideas for whole-school policies relating to attendance. Other related approaches, which can be adopted with staff and/or pupils, and have been effective in generating ideas for whole-school change are outlined below:

- describe a school which is ideal for truants, outlining the characteristics of the school, staff, pupils and parents.
- describe an ideal school which everyone would want to attend.
- ask staff to draw on their own experiences of school. Did they skip school? If so, why?
- ask staff to describe a school which is ideal for teachers.
- draw up a table to assist staff and pupils in considering the factors which encourage pupils to want to attend school (see below).

Things that encourage children to come to school	Things that make children not want to come to school

Questions of attendance cannot be considered without reference to the morale of school staff. The inter-relationships between the two are crucial. If staff themselves are demoralised or experiencing stress, they will find it difficult to commit themselves to improving the attendance of pupils. Individually, staff are often reluctant to raise such issues. Time set aside for their exploration might therefore be well spent.

Action

The processes outlined above will have generated many practical ideas for action. From these it is necessary to decide on priorities by selecting those changes which are most likely to be effective in markedly improving pupil attendance and which are perceived as achievable.

These decisions need to be arrived at in full consultation with all staff to ensure their commitment to the initiatives which are implemented.

Do not be over ambitious. Select a small number of ideas to start with. As these are implemented evaluate their effect. On the basis of these evaluations further action can be taken. Chapter 7 explores issues relating to evaluation.

Implications for staff training

Schools need to be aware that both teaching and non-teaching staff may require training. Likely training requirements are outlined in each section of the book.

Training is most beneficial when it is planned within a coherent framework. Unrelated sessions are less likely to be effective in changing attitudes and practice. Training relating to attendance issues, at the individual and group level, is best incorporated into the school's overall development plan. High levels of motivation are usually achieved when staff have been involved in decisions regarding the training they are to undertake.

Staff undertaking higher degrees may wish to explore issues relating to attendance as part of their studies. This can be mutually beneficial, the school providing a receptive environment for research, which in turn provides valuable information for the school.

4 Raising awareness and generating ideas for change

Summary

The importance of attendance at school needs to be raised in school and with the local community. To achieve this, use can be made of:

- the media;
- social and artistic events;
- information displayed in school;
- leaflets and letters to parents;
- local industry and commerce.

The process of generating ideas for change is important to establish commitment
from those who will be affected.

Pupils, teachers, and ancillary staff need to be directly involved.

The involvement of governors, parents, EWOs, counsellors, Education Psychologists, representatives of other agencies, the local community, industry, and commerce will also be beneficial.

Ideas can be generated through the use of:

- questionnaires;
- targeted discussion;
- brainstorming;
- specific activities.

A small number of ideas from those generated should be selected for action.

Schools need to be prepared to make provision for staff training.

SECTION II
SETTING UP
POLICIES AND
PROCEDURES

5 Day-to-day management of attendance

Schools need to develop efficient and effective procedures for monitoring and following up absence. Adopting effective procedures not only enables accurate monitoring but can promote attendance by acting as a deterrent. If pupils know that they will be found out if they skip lessons or school some will refrain from doing so.

This chapter outlines a number of procedures relating to the recording and follow up of absence, which have been effective in schools nationwide. They may provide ideas for developing appropriate systems for your school. It is important to take account of factors particular to your school and its community. For instance, a split-site school may present special problems relating to communication. Some school communities may present challenges because of diverse language usage or poor literacy skills.

Effective administrative procedures include:

- registers;
- computer systems;
- categorising and coding absence;
- registration procedures;
- procedures for when a child is absent;
- lesson attendance;
- staff responsibilities;
- rewarding good attendance;
- organisation of work experience, staff days, etc.;
- staff training.

The staff involved in developing new procedures should be those who will be actively involved in their use. This is likely to include heads of year, form tutors, office staff and those from agencies outside the school, e.g. EWOs. Discussions relating to the monitoring of lesson attendance should also include subject teachers. Developing procedures for monitoring lesson attendance is particularly important as it places the onus for ensuring good attendance on all staff, not only those with a pastoral role.

▬ Recording half-day attendance

If schools are to improve attendance they must have accurate and systematic ways of recording it. They need to know their current attendance pattern. This acts as the starting point for assessing improvement. There are also legal requirements relating to recording attendance which schools must satisfy (see Section VI).

Attendance registers or computer systems are important tools for accurately identifying and keeping track of pupils' attendance over the school year. The recording of information must be accurate and reliable as it forms an important part of the evidence in the event of the prosecution of parents, or in the seeking of an Education Supervision Order (ESO). Records of attendance are legal documents. They can be challenged in court. They are an important element in the assessment made in any single case and in deciding the action to be taken.

New attendance regulations also require that statistics be kept on individual and group performance.

To achieve these ends the attendance register itself must enable easy and accurate recording of information.

▬ Registers

Registers are the traditional means of keeping attendance records and if accurately and consistently completed they provide perfectly satisfactory information.

To ensure that all staff are consistent in their completion of registers, some schools have found it useful to preface registers with a brief account of the legal requirements relating to pupil attendance, together with a list of agreed symbols for indicating the reason for absence and guidance on the production of registration figures.

Registers are legal documents and can be required in court in the event of legal proceedings. Members of staff can also be called upon to verify the evidence. Prosecution of parents for the non-school attendance of their child is no longer a civil but a criminal offence and has to be proved 'beyond reasonable doubt' instead of on a 'balance of probabilities'. When registers are requested as evidence for court proceedings, it is more likely that their accuracy will be challenged. For this reason, if a mistake is made on a register, and an alteration is necessary, it is important that this is explained in writing at the appropriate place on the register. Correction fluids should not be used in any circumstances.

In response to the increased detail required in recording absence some LEAs and schools have redesigned registers. For instance they have:

- Introduced alternate shading of lines to prevent mistakes in recording and scrutiny;
- Included fewer weeks on each page to give more space to record information;
- Included sections for recording home borough district, ethnic group, home language, date of birth, and any other additional information felt to be useful;
- Provided updated information and guidance for completing the register on the inside cover;
- Included the authorisation codes on the inside cover or at the edge of the page;
- Provided plastic jackets to retain the appearance of the register in case it needs to be used in court;
- Provided an envelope attachment to hold notes from parents when children are absent.

Computer systems

Many schools have found that computerisation has simplified the process of collating and presenting information on attendance. It enables the speedy organisation and analysis of data, which facilitates accurate monitoring of patterns of attendance at the individual, class, and school level. The ready availability of this information in an easily understandable form, can certainly be useful to schools in developing strategies for reducing absenteeism. But the installation of a computer system, on its own, will not improve attendance at school.

If computer systems are installed staff will require training in their use. Some 'teething' problems should also be expected. The school also needs to devise contingency plans should the computer system malfunction.

Because of the possibility of attendance records being used in court, certain safeguards are required in relation to the recording and printing out of computerised information. The regulations for registers require that the original entry in a register and any subsequent correction should be clearly distinguishable. The original entry itself cannot simply be amended. Where computer systems are used, the original entry and the correction should both be preserved in such a way that on printing the entries appear in chronological order.

In cases where computer print-out is retained as the attendance register, as soon as practicable after the end of each school year the sheets must be bound into annual volumes and left intact for a period of not less than three years. Schools using computers for attendance registration must make a print-out of the attendance register at least once a month. A print-out must also be made of the computerised admission register not less than once a year.

If the school decides to introduce a computerised system of registration, the governing body will also be required to register with the Data Protection Register as a data user under the 1984 Data Protection Act.

Whether schools decide to make use of new technology or continue to use traditional registers, they will still be faced with the task of categorising absence.

▓▓ Categorising absence

Schools are now required to classify absence as authorised or unauthorised. While the DFEE have provided guidelines to assist schools (see Section VI), they still have some freedom of interpretation within the categories. This involves making value judgements about the appropriateness of absence. Schools may have to verify the explanations given for absence.

The categorisation of absence has particular significance for the prosecution of parents and applications for Education Supervision Orders. All schools are legally required to report to their LEA continuous absences of more than two weeks and pupils who fail to attend regularly, unless the absence is covered by a medical certificate. LEAs have a duty to follow up cases of unauthorised absence. But parents will not be prosecuted, i.e. an offence will not be committed if it can be demonstrated that:

- the pupil was absent with leave;
- the pupil was ill or prevented from attending by any unavoidable cause;

- the absence occurred on a day exclusively set aside for religious observance by the religious body to which the pupil's parents belong;
- the school where the child is registered is not within walking distance of his or her home, and that no suitable arrangements have been made by the local authority or the funding authority for
  i) the child's transport to and from school
  ii) boarding accommodation
  iii) the child to become registered at a school nearer his or her home.

A limited defence is also available to the parents of traveller children.

Absence with leave

It is the school's responsibility to grant absence with leave. Leave can be granted in a number of circumstances. These are outlined below.

Special occasions

Parents have the right to withdraw their children from school to participate in a day set aside exclusively for religious observance in the family faith. Schools can, at their discretion, also give permission for students to be absent for special occasions, in relation to family bereavements and for family holidays and extended trips overseas. The detailed criteria pertaining to such decisions are laid down by the DFEE (See Section VI). Decisions made by the school ultimately depend on value judgements made about the particular activity. Schools may have to reach decisions regarding a variety of activities. Examples are given below:

- A three-week holiday with parents;
- An extended visit for six months abroad to visit relatives;
- Meeting relations visiting from abroad;
- Visiting a grandmother, who lives some distance away, on her 90th birthday;
- Taking part in a skateboarding competition;
- Taking a ballet examination;
- Representing a region in a national or international competition (sports, music, chess, etc.);
- Attendance at a job interview for part-time Saturday work.

Domestic circumstances

Schools have discretion in granting leave of absence for pupils to mind the house and look after brothers and sisters. While the guidelines specify that this should only be authorised in *exceptional* circumstances, it is left to the school to define these. This also applies to shopping trips. Some examples which may be useful for generating discussion in staff training are provided below:

- After a pupil has been away for three days a note is brought saying that she has been looking after younger siblings as their mother has a bad cold.

- After a family car accident, when both parents are hospitalised, a relative requests that a child be given permission to miss school for one day to look after other children in the family, while longer term care is arranged.

- A mother requests that her son be allowed to accompany her on a shopping trip to the city centre to buy sports kit, on the only day when her husband is available to take them by car.

- A father requests that his daughter regularly be allowed to be late on Mondays while she waits for paid help to arrive at home at 9 a.m. to look after her mother, who is crippled with arthritis.

▇ Authorising absence after it has occurred

When a parent offers an explanation for absence it is for the school to decide whether or not to accept it and authorise the absence. The decision can be taken by any person authorised to do so by the governing body.

If a child brings a note from home saying that he or she has been ill, or providing an alternative explanation, the school has to come to a decision about the legitimacy of the explanation and perhaps the legitimacy of the communication itself. Should the note, however dubious its authenticity or contents, be accepted by the school as appropriate for authorising absence? Given the current scrutiny of unauthorised attendance figures, schools might be forgiven for accepting notes at face value. But this may not be in the best interests of the child. Such decisions are likely to present schools with considerable moral dilemmas.

Lateness

The DFEE provide guidance on attendance in relation to lateness. Normally when students are up to 30 minutes late they are recorded as present at school. After this time the absence is recorded as unauthorised. However, it is for schools themselves to decide how tightly these criteria will be adhered to. They are still empowered to overlook lateness if there are particular difficulties at home or other genuinely unavoidable circumstances.

Coding different kinds of absence

Whether the school is using a computer system or registers, codings for different types of absence have to be used. Some computer systems may have already specified codings. As school registers are legal documents, the codes used must be clear and adopted consistently by those taking the register.

The DFEE (circular 11/91) suggest use of the symbols outlined below, although LEAs have the freedom to devise their own, provided that the necessary information is recorded, and authorised and unauthorised absences are clearly distinguished.

B	receiving part-time or temporary education at an off-site unit or other than at the school where registered
C	other circumstances (to be specified)
E	excluded (fixed or permanent pending confirmation by the governors)
H	annual family holiday (for which leave has been granted in advance)
I	attending interview
M	medical/dental
P	approved sporting holiday
R	day of religious observance
S	study leave
V	educational visit
W	work experience

An example is given below of an alternative system in use in one LEA. The information shown is included in the register, reminding tutors of good practice and the necessary codes.

Example from Croydon Education Authority

REGISTERS ARE A LEGAL DOCUMENT AND MUST BE ACCURATE AT ALL TIMES

1. All Staff are asked to use the following procedure to standardise our practice.
2. All absences must be covered by a note from parents or a telephone call via PIC.
3. Up to October half-term, please send out HM/P$ (absence note) on the first day of absence.
4. Senior Teacher will deal directly with EWO and keep PGT's informed.
5. The following symbols are to be used:

   /   Present
   X   Late – after register is closed. Time to be put in space at side.
   B   Educated off site/interview
   C   Other authorised absence
   E   Excluded
   H   Annual family holiday (agreed)
   I   Illness
   L   Late – before register closes. Time to be put in space at side.
   M   Medical/Dental Appointments
   N   No reason yet provided for absence Unauthorised absence
   O   Unauthorised circumstances Unauthorised absence
   P   Parentally condoned absence
   R   Religious/Sporting/Cultural
   S   Study Leave
   T   Truancy
   V   Educational Visit
   W   Work Experience
   Y   Enforced Closure

6. Registers are to be marked in RED for present and O in BLACK.
7. Symbols in black O to be in red.
8. Unauthorised absences are deemed as truancy.
9. At the start of a visit the organiser must leave a list of names of pupils who have gone on the visit with PIC.
10. On return from a visit, the visit organiser is responsible for placing a list of pupils present and absent from the visit in the appropriate registers.
11. PGT's must ensure that registers are brought up to date that day.
12. TIPPEX IS NOT TO BE USED.

    (Neat alterations with notes to explain any errors are to be made.)

WE ARE EXPECTED TO HAVE A 90% ATTENDANCE RATE, and our attendance figures can be published.

Registration procedures

In addition to the actual recording of absence, the procedures adopted for registration may require change.

Some schools have found it useful to draw up an attendance timetable. This will depend on the nature of the registration system in use. Devising such a timetable is useful as it provides a clear framework within which staff can work. An example is given below.

Attendance timetable

8.15 onwards	Phone lines are manned for parents to ring in reporting absence
9.00	Pupils report for registration
9.05 to 9.30	Pupils arriving late sign in giving their reasons for lateness
9.30	Registers to be returned to office
10.00	Office staff contact by telephone the parents of any child absent from school, where no message has been received.

Each member of staff is sent an absence list for the day so that they can check lesson attendance.

1.50	Pupils report for registration
1.55 to 2.20	Pupils arriving late sign in giving their reason for lateness
2.20	Registers to be returned to office
2.30 to 4.00	Office staff collate all records, noting any absence which is unaccounted for and informing the form tutor.

What is important is that the procedures adopted in the registration process are clear. Staff must be familiar with them and adopt them consistently. Responsibilities also need to be clearly defined.

Those staff who are involved in the registration process need to be given opportunities for providing feedback about the current system, its strengths and weaknesses. This can then be used as the basis for making changes.

It is particularly important that staff responsibilities are clearly defined and that there are systems in place to deal with times when staff are ill. If the functioning of the computer system depends on one member of staff, illness of that individual can have a devastating effect. If registration procedures are ineffective, or disrupted by absence there are also implications for safety. The school should have an accurate record, at all times, of every person who is on the premises. Procedures for monitoring personnel in this way also improve security in the school.

Included is an example of specified registry responsibilities derived from John Smeaton Community High School, Leeds. Broader staff responsibilities relating to the follow up of absence will be considered later.

▇ Absence procedures

Whatever system of following up absence is adopted it must meet the needs of those responsible for the task. Staff working on a daily basis in such a capacity are often able to make positive suggestions for improvement on the basis of their experiences. The system also needs to be standardised and structured so that all staff operate in the same way.

▇ Contact from parents

First, a decision needs to be made regarding the way that parents will contact the school when their child is ill. Traditionally, pupils have brought a note from their parents on their return to school, explaining the reason for their absence. The disadvantage of this approach is the length of time which can elapse before the school realises that the pupil is not ill and that the absence is unauthorised. Where pupils are reluctant to attend school this delay can allow habits of poor attendance to develop unchecked.

Ideally schools should request that parents contact them on the first day of absence, by telephone, personally, or with a letter or note. Of these, telephone contact may be the most practical. If telephone calls are to become the norm, schools should consider having additional phone lines installed so that parents are not constantly faced with an engaged line. Parents can also be requested to ring before a designated time when registers will be completed.

Office staff can be trained to take the calls and recognise those which are not genuine. If this system is adopted, calls should be carefully logged, with the pupil's name, the reason given for absence and the identity of the caller. These details can then be passed to the form tutor, or whoever carries out further follow-up procedures. They may already have knowledge of the family and be able to address problems immediately.

Where parents do not make contact on the first day as requested, the school can take immediate action. This prevents habits of non-attendance developing. Speedy action also indicates that the school cares when pupils do not attend.

Example from John Smeaton Community High School, Leeds

Registration Procedures for Student Registry

DAILY
* Read REGISTERS on OMR – am & pm
* NB any missing registers – to be followed up later
* Deal with any queries re missing marks
* Enter lates etc / enter other manual alterations from message sheets
* Remove 'Today's Absence' proforma from register for collection by YDs

MORNINGS
* Print out ABSENCE LIST – 13 copies
  to Year Directors / Staff Room / one copy for registry copies to – English, Maths, Art, Language, PE, Drama & Music area, Humanities, Science, Technology, Business Studies

WEEKLY
* Print out NEW REGISTER SHEETS – usually Thursday am
* Enter code on each sheet

FRIDAY MORNING
* When the registers have been read -
* Enter any further changes based on message sheets from Group Tutors
* READ ABSENCE REPORT SHEETS on the OMR
* Print out list of missing reasons for absence and give to Year Directors

FRIDAY AFTERNOON
* After reading registers and entering manual marks -
* PRINT OFFICIAL REGISTERS – including whole of present month
* In a new month – print this week plus one or two weeks of previous month
* Print-outs – send to YDs – who check and pass to Group Tutors
* PRINT WEEKLY ANALYSIS SHEETS – send to YDs for checking & distribution
* Put NEW REGISTER SHEETS in folders

MONDAY MORNING
* PRINT ABSENCE RECORD SHEETS (if not done on Friday pm)
* Enter sheet code number
* Place in Registers

OCCASIONAL
* Renew TELEPHONE MESSAGE SHEETS when necessary
* Check that REGISTER DETAILS Sheets are in registers
* Forward any editing to Receptionist

TERMLY/ YEARLY
* Print Registration Certificates and Termly or Yearly Analysis Sheets as required by Year Directors

REGULAR
* Printing of OFFICIAL REGISTERS
  – A final copy of the Official Register needs to be kept. To be printed when all (or most) of the reasons for absence have been entered e.g. after six weeks.

The school also needs to consider whether a child's absence will automatically be designated as authorised if a phone call or note is received from home. If not, under what circumstances will parental notes or calls be queried? In particular cases, where there is reason to doubt the authenticity of notes received from parents, the school may wish to keep records of the parents' signatures.

Examples of notes from parents

David Green   10/5/95   9.00 am.
Mother rang — will be late as his bike has been stolen and he is waiting for the police.

PH.

Jane Brown   14/9/95

Mother rang. Kept Jane at home to look after sister who is ill.

DH.

I wonder if it will be possible for Mark to have Friday to Tuesday off because Mark's relatives are coming from Glasgow. Mark has not seen them for TEN years. We would like him to spend some time with them as he might not have another chance to see them. I would be grateful.

thank you

 **School response**

To be effective a school's follow up to absence needs to be speedy and consistent. Pupils who are at risk of experiencing attendance problems need to be identified quickly. It is much harder to deal with the problem once non-attendance has become a habit.

Speed of response to absence

A prompt response by schools to unexplained absence has the effect of reducing the frequency and length of absences.

Contact can be made by letter or telephone. A response on the first day of absence is very effective.

Telephone calls have the advantage that they can be made immediately and cannot be intercepted by pupils. Where families do not have a telephone they are usually able to provide the number of a relative, friend or neighbour where they can be contacted. If schools decide to instigate immediate telephone contact when parents do not inform the school of their child's absence, there may be a period when telephone costs are high. These will decrease as parents and pupils adjust to the new system.

In the early stages of tackling attendance problems some schools, in conjunction with the Education Welfare Service, have organised immediate home visits by EWOs on the first morning of unexplained absence. Such 'blitz' visits are effective in the short term and serve to raise awareness in parents and pupils. But, the effects are not sustainable in the long term.

Consistency of response

To be effective the response from the school must be consistent. The follow up must be carried out in the same way for each pupil on every occasion of absence. A flow chart or set of absence procedures can be useful for demonstrating the relevant procedures and ensuring that they are undertaken consistently by all members of staff.

Where a child and his or her family do not respond to the school's initial action, the school will need to adopt further measures, for example:

- A handwritten first letter, from a person with whom the child is familiar, often their form tutor, usually gets a good response. Personal letters are better received than official letters, particularly those which are perceived to be standard computerised letters.

- Some schools after this initial stage prefer to make personal contact through a home visit, often working in conjunction with the EWO.

**Example of Absence Procedures from
John Smeaton Community High School, Leeds**

Absence Procedures

- If a pupil is absent at morning registration the Group Tutor will try to make contact with home unless a message about the absence has been received. This is particularly important in cases where the pupil's absence gives cause for concern on a regular basis.

- If it is not possible to contact home or the parent at work, then fill in the proforma 'Today's Absences'. It will be collected from the Student Registry by the Year Director or a member of the SMT and will be acted on if possible.

- The results of any contact with parents/carers etc. will be sent back to Group Tutors.

- Parents and pupils may be invited in to discuss any problems with the Year Director/Assistant. Whenever possible the Group Tutor should be included in these discussions. On some occasions the YD will cover a lesson for the Group Tutor so that the GT can meet with the family instead.

- There is always further support available from the SMT and in particular the Deputy Head (Pastoral).

- A series of letters is available from Year Directors/or on disk in the General Office to cover different problems:

  – concern over the number of broken weeks
  – concern that no reason has been received for absence
  – concern over the amount of absence
  – concern over punctuality

- There is also a series of letters available direct from the SIMS attendance module which are mail merged and addressed directly to the parent/carer.

- Every week there is a meeting between the Year Director and the EWO. Any necessary visits will be arranged. Pupils can be seen in school by the EWO. YDs will feed information back to Group Tutors.

- There should be a register check at the beginning of every lesson. Absence lists will be sent to each Area office so that a quick check can be made on missing pupils.

- There should be regular Internal Truancy Audits.

- Other schools have devised a series of phased letters, which are sent out at various times in a long period of unauthorised absence. Such letters explain procedures, invite parents to the school to discuss issues, inform parents when the case will be referred to EWOs and remind parents of their legal responsibilities and the possible penalties for non-attendance.

Example of a series of letters sent out from schools in Southwark

PHASED LETTERS: The following letters would be used on the mailmerge system, with information typed into the dotted areas specific to the case. The letters represent a formal phased intervention when an initial approach to the home by phone or hand-written letter has proved unsuccessful. Letter 6 is to inform parents of an unauthorised absence.

LETTER ONE

> Dear Mr and Mrs ....
>
> I am concerned to see that (child)'s attendance has not improved, in spite of my previous letter/phone call to you.
>
> This means s/he is missing a large part of the school week. If this continues, not only may s/he have difficulty catching up on lost work, but s/he may also lose contact with school friends.
>
> I need to talk with you to make sure (child)'s situation does not get worse. I will be free to see you at the following times:
>
> ....
> ....
>
> Please phone me to arrange the best time for you. I look forward to hearing from you.
>
> Yours sincerely,
>
>
> FORM TUTOR

LETTER TWO

> Dear Mr and Mrs ....
>
> I have written to you about my concerns over (child)'s attendance, but unfortunately, have had no reply to my letter.
>
> His/her attendance has not improved. If we do not talk to deal with the obvious problems (child) is having, I will have to pass this on the the Head of Year.
>
> I will be free to see you at the following times: ....
> ....
>
> Please phone me to arrange an appointment. I look forward to seeing you.

LETTER THREE

Dear Mr and Mrs ....

I am writing to invite you to a meeting in school to discuss
(child)'s attendance, which I believe has shown no improvement,
even though (form tutor) has written to you and asked you to
come in and discuss it. I have spoken to (child) who said that

....

I am sure (form tutor) has already pointed out to you the
importance of being in school every day, not only to keep up
with the work, but also to strengthen friendships and social
skills. I must remind you that you have a legal responsibility
to send your child to school and when you enrolled at (school)
you agreed to abide by this.

As I am unable to visit you at home, I must once again urge you
to come in to school to discuss this situation so that we may
make some plans together to improve (his/her) overall attendance
and ensure (s/he) is more settled in school.

I will be free at the following times:

....

Please phone to let me know when you are arriving, or come into
the school office and ask for me.

If I do not hear from you I will be consulting the Education
Social Worker who is Southwark Education's representative on
attendance.

Yours sincerely

HEAD OF YEAR

LETTER FOUR

Dear Mr and Mrs ....

As I have not heard from you, I have discussed (child)'s poor attendance with the school's Education Social Worker. She has agreed to see you in school, and we have arranged this for ......

The Education Social Worker's role is to support you in sending your child to school every day. She will be able to advise you at the meeting and we all hope to make (child)'s return to school as successful as possible.

I must remind you that it is your legal duty to ensure your child attends school regularly and if a formal referral is made to the Education Social Worker, it may well result in court action and £1000 fine for non-attendance.

I look forward to meeting you on the date above, so that we may make plans to ensure that legal action is avoided.

Yours sincerely

HEAD OF YEAR

**REFERRAL TO EDUCATION SOCIAL WORKER
LETTER FIVE**

Dear ....

I was disappointed to see that you were unable to attend the appointment made with the Education Social Worker in school.

As I have not heard from you, I am afraid you leave me with no alternative than to make a referral to the Education Social Work Service. I should point out that this is the first stage in a legal process which could result in court action and a fine of up to £1000 per parent for failing to ensure your child's attendance.

The referral form will include any information on (child) which I feel would be useful to the ESW, and I am now inviting you to come into school and discuss what is written about him/her. If you do not accept this invitation, I will go ahead without your comments, and will send a copy of the referral form to you in due course.

From now on I will be following the advice of the ESW and I will continue to send you information on (child)'s attendance if necessary.

Please feel free to phone at any time if you would like to make an appointment to see me.

Your sincerely

HEAD OF YEAR

**UNAUTHORISED ABSENCE
LETTER SIX**

Dear ....

I have received your note/phone message regarding (name)'s absence on (date).

I am afraid that I have to inform you that this is not considered an acceptable reason for absence (see below), and I am therefore leaving it unauthorised in the register.

As all unauthorised absence is now recorded on a pupil's records and end of year reports, I hope there will be no absences of this kind in the future.

Yours sincerely

FORM TUTOR

AUTHORISED AND UNAUTHORISED ABSENCE

The law authorises certain categories of absence; these are when a child is absent:

      - when prevented from attending by **sickness, or any unavoidable cause*;**

      - on any day exclusively set apart for religious observance by the religious body to which the parents belong;

      - on the grounds that suitable transport has not been provided and the school is not within walking distance.

*Unavoidable cause means something directly involving the child, and not other members of the family.

▓▓▓ Contact with pupils who are absent

If a school is aware that a child is going to be absent for several weeks, e.g. through illness or school refusal, they can attempt to maintain contact with the child to facilitate a successful return to school. This may be undertaken on a weekly basis, by telephoning to see how they are, sending a card from the class, sending a class newsletter, or encouraging visits from class members or teachers. Schools should also set work for long term absentees. Such procedures will help the pupil to feel that they have a place in the school and can reduce the stress on their return.

Example of a get well card

Procedures for lateness

Schools need to develop internal systems for dealing with pupils who are late for registration or lessons. The procedures should be set down clearly and used consistently. Pupils and parents need to be made aware of them.

If pupils are consistently late for school, it is more effective to discuss the causes of the problem with them and develop strategies for improving their time keeping, rather than punishing them. Punishment alone is rarely effective in changing behaviour.

The registration procedures for children who are late need to be clearly established. This is particularly important because of the implications for safety procedures.

Lesson attendance

Developing effective systems for monitoring lesson attendance is vital for improving school attendance. Skipping lessons is the most common form of non-attendance and if it goes undetected can lead to a deterioration in general attendance. Rigorously checking lesson attendance involves all staff and serves to make attendance a whole-school problem.

A number of procedures for monitoring attendance at lessons can be adopted:

- Taking a register for every lesson (to be effective this MUST be checked against an absence list)
- Having random checks on lesson attendance (fairly frequently)
- Monitoring particular students who are known to 'bunk off'
- Patrolling school premises

All of these are very effective if they are undertaken conscientiously.

Where lesson registers are to be checked against the day's absentees, teachers find it helpful if they are each given a written list of absentees. If thorough checking is not undertaken pupils will take advantage of the situation.

Often, when pupils miss individual lessons they do not leave the school premises. If schools can identify the places where they congregate and regularly check them this will also act as a deterrent.

Some schools have installed systems for computerising lesson registration. This often involves teachers filling in a computer sheet, although some systems work on swipe cards. Observations made by schools who have adopted such systems are outlined on the next page.

Lesson attendance can be monitored equally effectively by traditional methods, although the collating of information on a school-wide basis is then much more complex.

Monitoring lesson attendance can in some circumstances create conflict for teachers. The absence of disruptive students from lessons improves the teaching environment. Teaching smaller groups enables more individual attention to be given to the remaining pupils and serves to increase resources. Where pupil attendance is erratic, they require help in catching up with work. This reduces the time the teacher

---

Advantages and disadvantages of using computer systems

Advantages

- Every pupil is tracked throughout each day clearly indicating if a lesson is missed;
- Feedback is quick enabling a fast response to absence;
- Pupils realise that they can no longer avoid detection;
- Attendance at lessons improves;
- Daily patterns of attendance can be studied;
- Attendance at particular lessons can be monitored;
- Timetabling problems can be identified;
- Subject teachers become closely involved in the monitoring of attendance;
- Attendance moves from a pastoral to a whole-school responsibility;
- Form tutors see the information as useful.

Disadvantages

- Setting up computer systems is a complex, time-consuming task;
- Computer systems can be unreliable;
- Some systems are time consuming to use;
- Where swipe cards are utilised, pupils tend to lose their cards;
- Some teachers may feel anxious about operating computer systems;
- Monitoring lesson attendance closely may create anxiety for some teachers.

---

can spend with the rest of the class. For these reasons teachers may tacitly condone the absence of some pupils and it may go unreported. Schools need to recognise these difficulties. While adopting a whole-school approach to improving attendance will alleviate them in the long term, in the short term teachers may require additional support. This may include the provision of a learning support teacher, lunch-time classes, or training in coping with exceptionally difficult behaviour.

Staff responsibilities

Many of the decisions regarding attendance procedures involve designating staff responsibilities. If these are clearly established and staff know:

- what they need to do
- when they need to do it
- how to do it
- to whom they are responsible

then the system should function smoothly.

If mechanisms for giving checks, and feedback are also built into the system, then improvements can be made as necessary (see example below).

WEEKLY REGISTER CHECK

TUTOR GROUP   DATE

Please note the following marked items

☐   Insufficient, unclear or no information recorded for the following absence(s) ....
....
....
....

☐   Register needs to be returned to school office.

☐   Incorrect authorisation codes being used.

☐   Weekly totals not entered.

☐   Using incorrect colours/pencil/'tippex'

☐   Register needs repair

☐   Perfect. Well done.

☐   Other (see below).

Head of Year _____   ESW _____

Derived from Southwark Council.

Responsibilities need to be established in relation to the following broad categories:

- recording of attendance data;
- collation of attendance data;
- communication of attendance information to staff, governors and parents;
- follow up of absence;
- liaison with outside agencies;
- staff support and training.

There are many different ways that these responsibilities can be allocated. Some suggestions are made below.

Overall responsibility

While the governors and head have ultimate responsibility for attendance, the day-to-day management of pastoral care and attendance matters is usually undertaken by a senior member of staff, e.g. a deputy. Their responsibilities might include:

Pastoral care

- overall responsibility for pastoral care in the school;
- overall responsibility for staff support structures;
- career development and training of pastoral care staff;
- ensuring that pastoral care meetings are held regularly.

Attendance matters

- responsibility for collating attendance statistics;
- responsibility for developing and monitoring policy and practice in relation to attendance, both half-day and lesson attendance;
- responsibility for communicating information about attendance to governors, staff, parents and the community;
- responsibility for ensuring that all staff are aware of attendance policy and practice;
- dealing with staff development and training in relation to attendance;
- responsibility for the work of ancillary staff in relation to attendance;
- ensuring that key posts are covered and establishing absence procedures in the event of staff illness.

Heads of Year, Special Educational Needs Co-ordinators

Heads of Year and Special Needs Co-ordinators often take particular responsibility for following up cases of persistent absenteeism and dealing with day-to-day problems arising in relation to attendance:

- Making direct contact with parents regarding attendance, whether it is good or poor;
- Following up non-attendance at lessons in conjunction with subject teachers;
- Identifying at risk pupils and setting up appropriate intervention programmes;
- Working with persistent absentees;
- Supporting form tutors;
- Developing close communication with:
  Education Welfare Officers
  Other outside agencies
  Counselling services;
- Providing a directory of back-up services, e.g. support groups for child carers, traveller children, dyslexics, which can be made available to staff, parents and pupils when required.

To undertake these functions effectively Heads of Year and Special Needs Co-ordinators need to be available at times when staff or pupils can make contact with them easily, i.e. lunchtime, breaktime and immediately before and after school.

Form tutors

Historically, there has been a tendency for the form tutor to be undervalued. But in most schools, they have a key role to play in improving attendance, through the development of positive, supportive and continuing relationships with the students in their tutor group. To undertake this role effectively, they require training and support, adequate time to undertake their duties and an acknowledgement of the importance of their work.

Their role is likely to include:

- Acquiring detailed knowledge of the individuals in their tutor group;
- Developing trusting and continuing relationships with those pupils;

- Monitoring their attendance, progress, behaviour and achievement;
- Arranging for credits to be given for good attendance, progress, behaviour and achievement;
- Monitoring diaries for homework, attendance, etc.;
- Advising colleagues regarding their progress, achievement, etc.
- Following up individual cases of absence;
- Providing support when pupils return to school after a long absence;
- Liaising with EWOs, the home and other agencies.

Practices which have proved successful in promoting the development of effective tutoring skills include:

- Heads of Year working closely with tutors;
- Cover being provided by the Head of Year for some tutorial sessions to enable tutors to interview individual students;
- Time being set aside for tutors to undertake tutorial work when they are not expected to provide teaching cover;
- The work of tutors being monitored to ensure consistency and vigilance;
- New staff being allocated to assist successful form tutors so that they can acquire the necessary skills.

Subject teachers

As Section III of the book illustrates, pupils often skip school because they are experiencing difficulties with their work, or in their relationships with teachers or peers. If a school is committed to improving attendance, they must address these issues. This requires the adoption of a whole-school approach, which raises the status of subject teachers in promoting attendance.

Subject teachers have an administrative role to play in monitoring and dealing with non-attendance in their lessons. They should be supported in this by the provision of appropriate procedures in the school.

Subject teachers and the departments within which they work also need to develop ways of helping pupils catch up with work when they have been absent. The most effective way of achieving this is to develop learning materials which can be worked on independently, with additional support being provided at lunch time, break or after school. Building up a bank of such resources might be undertaken jointly with the home tuition service, or other schools. Some LEAs have seconded teachers for such initiatives. These materials can be used by pupils if they are away from school for any reason, e.g. illness, exclusion, traveller children.

Subject teachers have a role in feeding information back to form tutors. This might relate to any aspects of the pupil's attendance, behaviour, progress, or achievement, positive or negative.

They also have a responsibility to act on information received from the form tutor. This might be related to difficulties the pupil is experiencing at home or school, information about health, etc. or information about a child returning to school. Readjusting to school after a long absence for any reason, can be difficult. All staff need to take care not to make insensitive remarks during this time as they may undermine the whole process of reintegration.

Subject teachers can also incorporate work on attendance into the curriculum.

Ancillary staff

Recently, with the increased use of information technology, office staff have taken on more important roles in relation to attendance issues. In some schools office staff:

- operate computer systems on a day-to-day basis;
- take phone messages when pupils are absent from school;
- make initial phone calls to parents when pupils are absent without explanation;
- send out computer generated letters;
- collate information from computer print-outs.

If office staff are to take on such responsibilities, the school must recognise that they may require training. It is also important for schools to establish clear boundaries between the responsibilities of form tutors and office staff.

Clarifying staff responsibilities

However administrative responsibilities are allocated, it is helpful for staff, if they are set out clearly, and in such a way that they can see how their work relates to that of others (see example below).

Attendance responsibility chart from
John Smeaton Community High School, Leeds

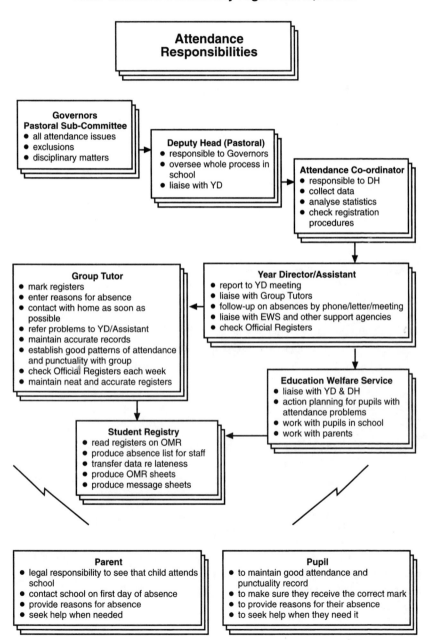

Attendance Responsibilities

Governors Pastoral Sub-Committee
- all attendance issues
- exclusions
- disciplinary matters

Deputy Head (Pastoral)
- responsible to Governors
- oversee whole process in school
- liaise with YD

Attendance Co-ordinator
- responsible to DH
- collect data
- analyse statistics
- check registration procedures

Group Tutor
- mark registers
- enter reasons for absence
- contact with home as soon as possible
- refer problems to YD/Assistant
- maintain accurate records
- establish good patterns of attendance and punctuality with group
- check Official Registers each week
- maintain neat and accurate registers

Year Director/Assistant
- report to YD meeting
- liaise with Group Tutors
- follow-up on absences by phone/letter/meeting
- liaise with EWS and other support agencies
- check Official Registers

Education Welfare Service
- liaise with YD & DH
- action planning for pupils with attendance problems
- work with pupils in school
- work with parents

Student Registry
- read registers on OMR
- produce absence list for staff
- transfer data re lateness
- produce OMR sheets
- produce message sheets

Parent
- legal responsibility to see that child attends school
- contact school on first day of absence
- provide reasons for absence
- seek help when needed

Pupil
- to maintain good attendance and punctuality record
- to make sure they receive the correct mark
- to provide reasons for their absence
- to seek help when they need it

▬ Communication between staff

In questions relating to attendance the importance of communication between staff at all levels cannot be overstated. Regular meetings of different groups of staff, where attendance issues are regular items on the agenda, will facilitate this. Subject teachers and pastoral care staff should be equally involved. The Education Welfare Officer working with the school can also be invited.

▬ Rewarding good attendance and punctuality

Some reservations have been expressed about rewarding good attendance at school. But handled sensitively, providing a reward system for good attendance and punctuality is not harmful and can help to improve both.

Where non-attendance is a major problem, the most effective systems to adopt initially are cumulative. Rewards are provided for short periods of time, e.g. two weeks. These can then be built upon increasing to half a term, a term and then a year. This gradual build up of rewards ensures self-monitoring, which can be assisted by the provision of log books or diaries for pupils to record their attendance, homework, etc.

Rewards can also be given for improved attendance. Some schools have introduced rewards for 97 per cent rather than 100 per cent attendance, to remove the anxiety and disappointment experienced by some pupils when they were unavoidably away from school and could not achieve 100 per cent. In addition to giving rewards to individuals, they can be given to classes, house groups, and year groups.

When introducing a reward system it is useful to canvas the views of pupils to establish those rewards which would be most popular. Involving pupils in the process of improving attendance, in this way, helps to generate increased commitment.

Those rewards which have found favour with students include stickers which can be placed in easily visible places, merit points, certificates to be included in Records of Achievement, letters to parents, tuck shop tokens, personalized prizes which are visible in school, e.g. inscribed pens or key rings, tokens which can be exchanged for goods, school prizes. School trips, particularly those which involve overnight stays, are valued rewards and also serve to strengthen group relationships which can also assist in improving attendance.

**Examples of certificates/letters rewarding
attendance and letter sent home to parents**

_____ *SCHOOL*

Certificate *of* Attendance

Awarded to

_____

for Excellent Attendance

_____ *HalfTerm 199*

signed _____ *Tutor*

_____ *Head of Year*

Attendance Award

Presented to

for

Date   Signed

HALING MANOR HIGH SCHOOL

Attendance Certificate

....

Has achieved 100% attendance this Term

Senior Teacher

Croydon Education Authority

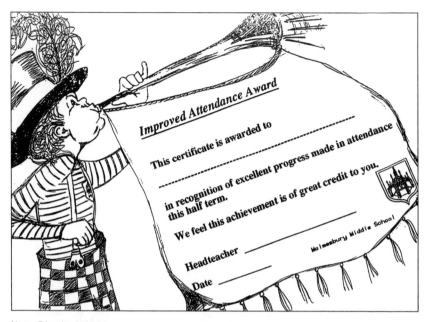

Merton Education Authority

March 1992

Dear Mr and Mrs Smith,

I am pleased to inform you that Suzy has just received a certificate for excellent school attendance.

We firmly believe that good attendance and punctuality is the basis for all other achievements.

In the partnership between the school, pupils and families the support you are giving your child to attend every day has immense value to her education.

This letter is to thank you for your support and to let you know that the school appreciates the value you put on full attendance.

Yours sincerely

Form Tutor

Example from Southwark Education Authority

As part of the reward process it is important to give attendance issues a high profile, for example:

- assemblies can be used as vehicles for rewarding and providing information about attendance;
- displays can be mounted at parents' evenings;
- schools can put up an attendance notice board displaying current information;
- LEAs can give public recognition to excellent school attendance or its improvement.

Organisation of work experience and holidays

Impending school holidays can bring about a fall in attendance. This tends to be greater with the increase in age of the pupils. Part weeks prior to holidays cause an even greater fall, especially when they occur at the end of the summer term.

Work experience and study leave taking place within a few weeks of a major holiday also disrupt attendance in those year groups involved. The greatest fall in attendance is noted when the activity finishes a week before the end of term. However, when timed appropriately, work experience and study leave improve attendance. Pupils' motivation appears to increase during these times, perhaps as a result of wanting to do well in examinations and realising the importance of education, having had experience of the work place.

The timing of staff training days is also important. Midweek training days cause the most disruption to attendance. The day which causes the least is Friday. To avoid pupils missing the same lessons on training days, the time table can be readjusted during these weeks so that it is not always Friday's lessons that are missed.

If there are unexpected problems during the year, e.g. extreme weather conditions, the effects on attendance are less detrimental when a positive decision to close the school is taken. If the school remains open, but only a few pupils attend, this can set a precedent for non-attendance, which for some pupils marks the beginning of a pattern of non-attendance.

■ Staff training

There are important implications for staff training in relation to the everyday management of attendance, for staff at all levels.

The training of form tutors requires a rolling programme to cater for staff new to the school. An 'apprenticeship' system can be adopted, where inexperienced staff work with successful tutors for a year. More formal training might also be required in relation to:

- the completion of registers;
- the categorisation of absence;
- recognising cases where letters from home are not authentic;
- follow up procedures;
- the law in relation to school attendance;
- positive attendance strategies;
- social and relationship building skills;
- effective communication with parents;
- making home visits;
- counselling.

Senior staff with responsibilities for attendance and pastoral care also need opportunities to update their knowledge, explore new ideas and develop better practice within the school.

5 The day-to-day management of attendance

Summary

For the effective day-to-day management of attendance schools need to:

- Develop appropriate systems for keeping detailed and accurate registration information;
- Develop and implement efficient and effective registration procedures;
- Adopt ways of promoting effective two way communication with parents and carers;
- Monitor patterns of half-day attendance;
- Monitor lesson attendance;
- Follow up non-attendance of any kind consistently and speedily;
- In consultation with pupils, develop and implement systems for rewarding good attendance and punctuality;
- Organise staff training, work experience and study leave to minimise disruption to attendance;
- Establish the most effective use of staff to implement the systems;
- Detail staff responsibilities clearly;
- Provide mechanisms for feedback;
- Provide resources for the task to be undertaken effectively;
- Provide resources for staff training.

6 Writing and communicating policy

Attendance policy in a school is based on the practices adopted by that school. Developing administrative, procedural and whole school practices, aimed at improving attendance will take account of the pattern of attendance of the school and the particular characteristics of the school community. As the school develops suitable strategies for dealing with them, attendance policy will evolve. Once policy is formulated it needs to be documented and communicated to pupils, parents, and other members of the school community.

Recent legislative changes require that governors are aware of and take responsibility for the attendance of pupils in their school. They are required to publish attendance rates in their annual report and the responsibility for ensuring that policy is adequately formulated, documented and communicated, ultimately lies with them.

Writing the policy document

The written policy needs to take account of the DFEE guidelines on attendance (see Section VI). The school may also wish to consider the criteria set out for OFSTED inspections. This states that Inspectors are to investigate the school's actions to improve attendance where attendance for classes or years falls below 90 per cent. Punctuality at the start of the school day and for individual lessons will also be considered.

The evidence used by OFSTED includes:

- Registers of attendance;
- Attendance statistics for the school, year groups and individual classes;
- Data on authorised and unauthorised absence;
- The school's policy and any other documentation on attendance including 'compact schemes', reward systems, and information to

parents and pupils regarding the school's expectations regarding attendance and the procedures for follow up of absence;

- Pupil records, including correspondence with home and the Education Welfare Service;
- Discussions with pupils and staff;
- Pupils' punctuality in arriving at school and in class.

Taking account of the DFEE guidelines and OFSTED requirements the written policy should clearly set down:

- the aim of the school in relation to attendance;
- parent's legal responsibilities in relation to school attendance and the responsibilities of the school;
- how absence will be categorised as authorised or unauthorised;
- the policy of the school for authorising absence in special circumstances, and how to apply for it;
- procedures by which parents should contact the school in case of absence;
- the procedures that the school will adopt in relation to the follow up of absence in the short and long term;
- the procedures for a child's return to school;
- the reward system for good attendance.

Aims

The policy document begins with a statement of expectations regarding attendance linked to the mission statement of the school. This will encompass the ethos and values of the school, and may also be explicitly linked to other school policies, e.g. bullying, special needs (these will be discussed more fully in Section III of the book). For example, an Oxford Middle School aims to:

> 'create a warm, welcoming and secure atmosphere where children feel valued; provide a stimulating and accessible curriculum delivered in a physically clean, bright and attractive environment'

Aim from the attendance policy of Bayswater Middle School, Oxford.

▌ Parental and school responsibilities

This section includes a description of what the school expects of pupils and parents and what they in turn can expect from the school. Parents' legal obligations must be outlined and schools may further specify that parents ensure that their child:

- is punctual;
- attends prepared to work;
- brings the correct equipment;
- completes homework.

They might also request that they be informed, in confidence, of any problems that the child is experiencing.

In return the school sets out what it is offering to parents and pupils, e.g. to provide a safe, secure environment, and education of a high quality, where attendance is monitored effectively and support is provided where necessary.

▌ Contact in case of absence

The policy should outline how and when parents should contact the school in case of absence, e.g. by telephone, personal contact or written note on the first day of absence.

▌ Categorisation and leave of absence

The document sets out the criteria for categorising absence as authorised or unauthorised and the circumstances under which the school will grant leave of absence (see Chapter 5). These must be framed within the DFEE guidelines. Parents should be given clear guidelines, although the school should allow for the possibility of discretion in certain cases.

Parents must also be familiarised with the procedures for applying for leave of absence, for instance, whether the request should in be writing, to whom it should be made and whether it has to be made several weeks before the event.

▌ School procedures for following up absence

Parents need to understand the procedures which the school will set in motion if their child is absent without authorisation. This, in turn, will be related to the way that parents themselves contact the school. For instance, if parents are requested to phone the school before 10.00 a.m. in the event of their child's absence, they need to know what will happen if they do not do this, e.g. the school will telephone them.

The policy should also set out the school's procedures in cases of prolonged absence, whether through illness or for unauthorised reasons.

▬▬ Procedures for return to school after a long absence

The written policy outlines the ways that a child will be supported by the school, on their return after a long period of absence (see Section V).

▬▬ Encouraging attendance

The written policy sets out the ways that the school will encourage punctuality and good attendance. This should include a description of the reward and penalty systems which are in operation, and information about how attendance records will be communicated to parents, e.g. letters, or school reports.

▬▬ Communication of policy

Once the policy document has been formulated, effective ways of communicating its contents to parents, within the wider framework of improving links with the home and the community (see Section IV), need to be considered. Parents and carers in the school community are unlikely to be an homogenous group and the communication may have to be undertaken in a number of different ways to ensure that it is fully understood. Some parents may have literacy difficulties, or be unfamiliar with the English language. Some will regularly attend meetings at school, while others will not. In some cases parents will be divorced or in the process of separation, which may present communication problems.

Attendance policy can be communicated through the school prospectus, in newsletters, at parents' evenings, and through PTAs, and local community groups. Schools might also consider:

■ the translation of leaflets into languages used in the local community;
■ using posters;
■ the use of humour;
■ the use of cartoons;
■ making a video cassette illustrating attendance issues.

Communication of policy will be an ongoing process as new pupils join the school.

Examples of letters and leaflets to parents illustrating attendance issues

Dear Parent,

I am writing to all parents* about the role you play in supporting your child's attendance.

One of the most important things affecting your child's progress at school is regular attendance. For your child to gain the most benefit from her or his education, it is important that you work in partnership with the school to encourage good attendance and also to confirm that you know about any absence.

Under normal circumstances, **the only reason children should miss school is if they are too ill to attend.** If this should happen, we would appreciate a message as early as possible by phone. When your child returns to school s/he should bring a note or you should phone again to explain the absence more fully. In the case of illness, this would be enough to **authorise** the absence in the register. You can then rest assured that if your child is away without any message from home, *the school will soon let you know of its concern!* In the case of frequent illnesses or a longer illness, a medical certificate may be requested.

If **any other circumstances** make it necessary for your child to miss a day then it is important that this is discussed with the Head of Year, who will then decide if the absence can be authorised. Please try to do this in advance so that the form tutor is always fully informed and knows when to expect your child back at school.

If information is not received from parents, then the absence will remain **unauthorised,** and the school will need to take steps to find out why the child has been away.

Another reason why it will remain unauthorised is if the reason given is thought not to be acceptable to the school, according to Government guidelines. These unauthorised absences now go down on a child's record and on their end of term reports.

Some parents are already keen to keep in touch and I am hoping to encourage this good communication between home and school. Please support us in our efforts to educate your child and to ensure that s/he is safely where s/he should be, **in school regularly and on time.**

If you have any worries or queries about this, please do not hesitate to contact the school at any time on the number above.

Yours sincerely,

Head Teacher

*Parents, carers and those with parental responsibility

Southwark Education Authority

WHY ...... SCHOOL WANTS YOU TO KEEP IN TOUCH

When your child is away from school for any reason, please could you be sure to let the form tutor known the reason as soon as possible, by phoning the school and/or writing a note to bring in on returning to school.

Please help us to help you ... this way we know your child is safe and where s/he is supposed to be ...

If we don't hear from you then you may hear from us ...

WE CARE ABOUT OUR PUPILS ATTENDING SCHOOL

Why We Encourage Good Attendance

.... School has one of the HIGHEST ATTENDANCE RATES in the Borough for a mixed school, with an average of 89%

This has a direct effect on the RESULTS and SUCCESSES of the pupils, which is why staff give such a high priority to ENCOURAGING GOOD ATTENDANCE

This Year's Year 7 has so far maintained an average attendance of 94% Many pupils will soon be receiving Certificates for 100% Attendance and punctuality.

★✿✤○✲✳✴✳✤○✱★

WE HOPE TO SUSTAIN THIS GOOD RECORD AND WE HOPE THAT PARENTS WILL HELP US BY GIVING THEIR CHILD EVERY ENCOURAGEMENT TO COME TO SCHOOL *EVERY DAY AND ON TIME...*

Southwark Education Authority

Malmesbury Middle School

16th November, 1994.

Dear Parent/Guardian,

Recently school attendance has become an important national issue and has been the subject of much research and debate, as you may have seen in the press and on T.V.

Through regular attendance pupils gain both educationally and socially, by taking part in school life with their classmates.

Whilst sickness is unavoidable in schools there is increasing concern over the minority of pupils whose attendance is punctuated by frequent one day or half day absences.

Where non-attendance occurs children miss valuable learning time, then it is often difficult for them to have a complete understanding of the work covered in the classroom.

Regular attendance and punctuality are important if your child is to gain the maximum from his/her education and develop good habits for the world of work.

As a school we have now become involved in the Merton Attendance Project, which means we will be giving the matter of attendance an even higher priority in school.

We hope to have sessions with the children to discuss attendance and its importance as well as award certificates for high attendance rates and good progress in attendance. Each child will also record his/her attendance on charts/graphs displayed in the classrooms. Many activities will be set up to involve the children in the issue of attendance.

We recognise that we all need to work together for the benefit of the children and the community; teachers, governors, welfare officers and most importantly, you, the parents. We hope that, with your cooperation, involvement and support we will be able to encourage, recognise and reward regular attendance within the school.

We thank you in anticipation of your cooperation.

Yours faithfully,

Ms. P. Woodhouse.

Project

London Borough of Merton

CRICKET GREEN SCHOOL

Lower Green West
Mitcham Surrey CR4 3AF

Dear Parents/Guardians

We would like to remind parents that they are required to contact school before 9.30am on the first day of their child's absence. Should we not hear anything then we will be contacting parents throughout the morning in order to confirm the reason for their absence.
We feel that it is important for school to know the exact whereabouts of each pupil in order to comply with the child protection act.

Also at the beginning of the spring term we are introducing an attendance record card for each pupil to fill in every day. We hope that it will encourage pupils to work towards receiving an attendance certificate at the end of each term.

Yours sincerely

D. Timmins
(Merton Attendance Co-ordinator)

John Sneaton
Community High School

Attendance Matters!

Smeaton Approach
Barwick Road
Leeds LS15 8TA
Tel (0532) 644251
Headteacher: G P Willis, B.Phil(Ed)

Why is good Attendance Important?

★ school work is easier to cope with
★ pupils feel more secure
★ work is more satisfying
★ better results
★ better job prospects

Rewards for Good Attendance

★ certificate and gift voucher for full attendance
★ certificates for 100% per term
★ certificates for attendance over 97%
★ entry in Record of Achievement
★ letters home

What can we do to help you?

★ If there is a problem please let us know.
★ The person to contact in school is :-

_____ (Group Tutor)

_____ (Year Director)

What can you do to help us?

★ If your child is absent please could you phone us on the first day of absence?
0532 644251

Name of pupil _____

Tutor Group _____

What is meant by Unauthorised Absence?

★ Some absences are allowed by law. For example if the child is ill or there is a family crisis such as a funeral. However, there are other times when pupils are absent which are not permitted.

★ We need the help of parents to cut down on this kind of absence.

Going to have their hair done!!

Looking after younger children or other relatives

Sleeping in!

Going out to buy shoes

Waiting in for the gas man or other tradesmen

Doing the Shopping

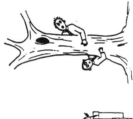

Having a birthday - some pupils think they should have a day off!

★ We realise that on some occasions there may be a particular problem that causes your child to be absent. Please let us know and we will deal with it sympathetically.

Truanting

Holidays

★ In recent weeks we have been concerned by the amount of school time that pupils have missed as a result of holidays with their parents.

★ Only 10 school days per year are allowed for this and we would urge you, if it is at all possible, to take your holiday during school holiday periods.

★ If pupils miss a two week spell of time from school it is very difficult for them to catch up with their work in an effective way.

★ Please let us know in advance if this loss of time is unavoidable.

City of Coventry

Gujerati

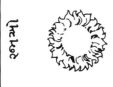

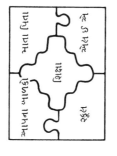

Parents appreciate information about the outward signs of non-attendance at school. When children skip school there is sometimes an assumption on the part of the school that the parents are aware of this and in some way condone it. Parents are often unaware of their child's absence from school. Children can become very adept at covering up non-attendance, leaving and returning home at the normal time, taking their school bag, even pretending to do homework. If schools do not inform parents of a pupil's non-attendance they may simply be unaware of it. Illustrated below is the kind of information they may find useful.

Signs of children not attending school

- a lack or knowledge and interest regarding anything connected with school;
- a sudden reduction in or lack of homework;
- few or no school communications;
- an interest in where parents will be during the day;
- friends who are known to skip school;
- a detailed knowledge of daytime TV programmes;
- attempts to keep their parents away from school events;
- a keenness to get to the post in the morning (to intercept letters from school).

To ensure that communications are effective, parents can be asked to give feedback on the presentation of information and make suggestions for ways it might be improved. This can be undertaken through the Parents–Teacher Association, by personal contact or through the design and distribution of a brief questionnaire.

6 Writing and communicating policy

Summary

Attendance policy is based on practices operating in the school and:

- Is devised in relation to accurate knowledge of the school's pattern of attendance;
- Reflects the characteristics of the school community.

The policy explains:

- The aims of the school in relation to attendance;
- Parents' legal responsibilities;
- How absence will be categorised as authorised or unauthorised;
- The criteria for granting authorised absence in special circumstances;
- The procedures for parents when their child is absent;
- The school's procedures when absence occurs;
- The school's procedures when pupils return to school after a long absence;
- The way that the school encourages good attendance and punctuality.

Schools should attempt to communicate the policy in ways which will be easily understood by the school community.

7 Monitoring and sustaining improvement

As policy and practice on attendance are developed within a school, systems for their monitoring and evaluation should also be set up. These should be an integral part of school procedures. The importance of this cannot be overstated. Patterns of absenteeism change over time, reflecting changes in the school community. To respond to this, attendance patterns need to be monitored over time and the effectiveness of policy and practice re-evaluated. Changes can then be made if circumstances indicate that it is necessary. Regular evaluations are also important in maintaining momentum, which is essential for improving attendance in the long term.

For evaluation to be carried out thoroughly and systematically, staff at varying levels must be made responsible for its undertaking and for reporting the findings to meetings of staff and governors.

Sustaining improvements in attendance

In the short term it can be relatively easy to improve attendance. While attendance is under scrutiny, designated as requiring improvement, and included in the school development plan, perhaps with additional funds being made available, staff and pupils are likely to be well motivated. Once this initial interest wanes, it is easy for old patterns of behaviour to return. Maintaining the momentum is difficult. If the school builds in procedures for the continued monitoring and evaluation of policy and practice, commitment is more likely to be maintained.

The kinds of procedures that schools have found helpful include:

- A regular time each week when pupils fill in their attendance homework cards;
- Regular reviews of attendance between form tutors and pupils as part of Records of Achievement;

- School attendance as a topic for school assembly, Personal–social Education lessons, themes in Maths, English, Humanities, Music lessons, etc.;
- The means for pupils to become familiar with the work of EWOs, e.g. involving EWOs in staff training sessions, Personal–social Education lessons, school outings, extra curricular activities, etc.;
- Displays of attendance information in prominent places;
- Regular communication with parents on attendance issues (as described earlier);
- Repetitions of initial communications regarding attendance to the parents of children new to the school;
- Procedures where regular reports are made regarding attendance at meetings of governors, year group staff, the full school staff.

Difficulties in improving attendance have been found relating to:

Procedures

- inaccurate marking of registers
- out-of-date or incomplete pupil information
- unchecked lesson attendance
- lack of time for the support and monitoring of pupils experiencing difficulties
- lack of consistency in the implementation of school policy

Curriculum and teaching

- the curriculum and its delivery have been inappropriate

Staff commitment

- pressured middle and senior management
- low staff morale following reorganisation or the introduction of major new initiatives
- stressed staff through covering for absent colleagues
- staff reluctant to accept responsibility for improving attendance
- difficulty or reluctance by staff to make contact with pupils' homes on the first day of absence
- poor teacher–pupil relations
- lack of sensitivity and support by staff for pupils, particularly those returning after a long absence

---

Derived from the Leeds Attendance Project

A number of factors have been found to have a negative effect on attempt to improve school attendance and sustain it over time. The Leeds attendance project revealed a number of crucial features. These are outlined in the box on page 93.

▇ Evaluating the effectiveness of policy and procedures

The evaluation of new policies to discourage absenteeism can be divided into four areas which reflect the structure of this book, that is:

1 procedures;
2 factors within the school;
3 factors outside school;
4 strategies for working with absentees on an individual basis.

The essence of evaluation is to establish whether the procedures and practices are working effectively. On the basis of this feedback future plans can be made.

The effectiveness of attendance policy and practice cannot be assessed without reference to other measures of school effectiveness. If pupils are attending school regularly there should be an improvement in measures of achievement. Changes in the social climate of the school will be reflected in changes in behaviour. Improvement in relations with parents and the wider community may in the long term lead to an increase in the number of parents wishing their child to attend the school. Statistical information will be important but there is also a place for feedback of a qualitative nature from staff, pupils and parents.

▇ Procedures

Staff involved in registration and procedures for following up absence should be given opportunities to discuss the effectiveness of those procedures and to make suggestions for improvement at regular meetings. Feedback relating to the monitoring of lesson attendance will need to be raised at full staff meetings.

▇ Factors within school affecting attendance

The effects of changes within the school can be established by gathering feedback from pupils, parents and outside agencies.

Pupils' views can be sought in tutor groups, the information being regularly fed back by form tutors to staff meetings. School councils can be set up which can represent the views of pupils. Pupils can also be represented on the governing body. Opportunities also need to be made for details of the meetings to be communicated back to the pupils in assemblies, tutor groups, or by newsletters. If communication is not two-way pupils may come to see the procedures as pointless.

Parents can also be a valuable source of information regarding the effectiveness of whole-school policies. Their views can be expressed through representation on the governing body, through the PTA, at parents' evenings and through written communication. Again, information regarding the reception of their feedback and any action to be taken should be communicated to them.

Outside agencies are an extremely valuable source of feedback regarding whole-school policies. EWOs, Educational Psychologists and School Counsellors are often privy to information from their referrals which can be invaluable in improving aspects of school functioning related to attendance. This can be communicated in ways which do not break confidences, and can be important in drawing attention to difficulties relating to bullying, racial harassment, drug use, curriculum difficulties, etc. Representatives from outside agencies can be invited to regular school meetings, providing opportunities for the exchange of information, which can be mutually beneficial.

Factors outside school affecting attendance

Progress in improving links with home and school can be evaluated with the help of community leaders, those working in the community, teachers from feeder primary schools, informal contact with parents, and representatives from local industry and commerce. It is also possible to acquire objective information regarding increases in:

- the number of parents attending meetings;
- the level of activity of the PTA;
- the number of community events being held in the school;
- the number of links made with feeder primary schools;
- the number of contacts made with local industry and commerce.

Although the quality of the links made is perhaps more important than their quantity, this can only be assessed on the basis of feedback from personal contact. However, the more frequent the contact, the greater the opportunity for developing better relations. An indication of increased contact might therefore be regarded as a positive sign.

■ Ways of working with absentees

In addition to concrete statistics detailing the numbers of pupils successfully returning to school after a long absence, the most important information for evaluating success in working with individuals will come from a consideration of case studies, successful and unsuccessful. Individual cases need to be analysed for common features. Failures should not be ignored. They can be more valuable in indicating ways of improving practice than successes.

Individual pupils can provide valuable feedback regarding the problems they have experienced and how the school might have helped more. This information can be collected by those who have supported pupils during their period of reintegration.

Suggested statistics for evaluating attendance policy and practice

Attendance and punctuality

- overall attendance figures;
- improvements in the attendance of year groups, particular classes or groups of children;
- reduction in the number of persistent absentees;
- an increase in the number of persistent absentees successfully reintegrated into school;
- improved lesson attendance;
- reduction in the number of pupils being late for school;
- improvement in being on time for lessons.

Achievement

- increase in the number of students taking examinations;
- improvement in examination performance;
- increase in the number of pupils continuing their education after 16.

Behaviour

- reduction in the number of exclusions from school;
- general reduction in the number of incidents of of recorded poor behaviour;
- reduction in the reported incidence of bullying.

Other professionals, e.g. counsellors, EWOs, working on individual cases also have valuable insights to contribute. Meetings of pastoral care staff provide an appropriate forum for such issues to be discussed.

▓ Statistical measures

Statistical information which might be included in an overall evaluation is outlined in the box on the previous page.

▓ Staff training

It is of crucial importance to evaluate the effectiveness of staff training. While most trainers seek immediate feedback on the effectiveness of the sessions that they provide, the real test of staff training is whether it brings about long-term change in ways of thinking or behaving. These outcomes are not observable immediately after training sessions.

▓ Action plans

Evaluation is only useful if it leads to action, where action is required. Often, when evaluations are undertaken, lengthy reports are written, recommendations are made and accepted but no action follows. Practices remain the same. If evaluation relating to attendance policy and practice is undertaken, any recommended action must be implemented if further improvement in attendance is to occur.

Subsequent to evaluation and appropriate consultation, an action plan should be drawn up, which should include: clearly defined aims, clearly defined staff responsibilities, time limits, criteria for success, and procedures for reporting outcomes. In this way the evaluation process becomes meaningful and useful.

7 Monitoring and sustaining improvement

Summary

- Appropriate mechanisms for evaluation need to be embedded within the school's attendance policy
- Staff responsibilities in relation to evaluation need to be clearly set out
- Reports on attendance and related issues should be made to governors, parents, and the whole-school staff

Evaluation should include:

- statistical information
- informal feedback from interested parties
- the effectiveness of procedures relating to:

   the everyday administrative arrangements for recording attendance and following up absence
   whole-school policies impacting on attendance
   links with parents, and the wider school community
   work with individuals
   staff training

Evaluation is only useful if it leads to appropriate action!

SECTION III
FACTORS WITHIN
SCHOOL AFFECTING
ATTENDANCE

8 Anxiety and school

When pupils are absent from school the reason most often given is illness. This is legally acceptable and on the surface seems simple and uncontroversial. Children soon realise that the only legitimate reason they can offer for not attending school is illness. If they wish to skip school for any reason they are likely to pretend to be ill. If anxiety is the cause of the problem their symptoms are likely to be genuine.

Anxiety and illness

Stressful situations create anxiety and can lead to illness. Children and adults commonly react to stress by producing physical symptoms. These often cannot be traced to physical causes.

If a child is ill, parents may have difficulty in deciding whether the symptoms have physical or psychological origins. Even if parents recognise that anxiety is the underlying cause of an illness, they may not know how to raise the problem with the school and find it simpler to just say the child is ill. Many parents feel uncomfortable raising issues which imply criticism of their child's school, especially if the problem centres around one teacher. They may be afraid that they will make matters worse and that life at school will be even more difficult for their child, if they complain.

Illness leading to unauthorised absence

If a child is absent from school for a long period of time or has a lengthy series of hospital or dental appointments the regular pattern of attendance will be broken. Teachers, the parents and the child come to accept non-attendance as the norm and this may continue when the illness is over and the appointments have ceased. The situation may be exacerbated if the child has problems catching up with missed work.

101

▐ Severe anxiety

In cases of extreme anxiety children may become what are commonly known as school phobics or school refusers. Such children experience severe emotional problems in relation to school attendance, although the underlying cause of their problem is often not related to school. They are likely to need additional help and support and may be referred to educational psychology or psychiatric services. These children represent a very small proportion of the school population. Estimates range from 0.4 per cent to 1.7 per cent of school-aged children.[8]

Case Study

Paul, an only child, is aged 13. He has enjoyed attending school and has found schoolwork easy. He and his family recently moved to a different part of the country because his father had a new job. After about three months of living there he had chicken pox followed by flu. This was near the end of the school year, immediately prior to the summer holidays. After the holidays he refused to go back to school. Now, when told to get ready for school he kicks, screams, shouts, swears and throws things. If he is not asked to go to school his behaviour returns to normal. On one occasion the doctor had to be called because he barricaded himself in his bedroom and refused to come out. Paul's distress is very real. His parents have always expected him to be obedient and until now this has been the case. They are extremely distressed by his behaviour.

■ *School refusal is not always related to problems at school.*

■ *Difficulties in school attendance can often be precipitated by transfer from one school to another and illness.*

▐ Anxiety and depression

In young people under the age of 25, suicide is the second most common cause of death. Although many of these suicides occur in young people beyond the age of compulsory schooling, there have been cases of suicide in children as young as 10. In recent years, there has been a 50 per cent increase in the number of children admitted to hospital with psychological problems. The organisation 'Young Minds' suggests that as many as 20 per cent of young people, about 2 million, have some kind of serious problem. While the causes of such problems are complex and multi-faceted, attendance and performance at school inevitably will be affected.

Causes of anxiety in school

Given the close relationship between anxiety and illness what may create anxiety in pupils at school? The main causes, as reported by pupils, fall under three headings:

- relationships;
- academic work;
- environment.

Although these are dealt with separately there is often overlap. Anxiety often has multiple causes.

Anxiety about relationships

Relationships at school include those with staff and peers. Difficulties with relationships can lead to anxiety and depression.

Relationships with teachers

When pupils are asked to give their reasons for non-attendance at particular lessons, the most common response is dislike of particular teachers. For instance, pupils dislike those who are sarcastic, make them feel stupid, and make remarks about their appearance. Anxiety is also created through fear of getting into trouble when work is not completed or not properly understood. Some pupils are genuinely afraid of some teachers.

Relationships with other pupils

Most pupils will at some time have disagreements with friends. For some young people these can be traumatic and may lead to a wish to avoid school. Relationship problems with peers at their most extreme may include bullying, or racial or sexual harassment.

Bullying

There has recently been a great deal of publicity about bullying in school and its effects. Bullying can take many forms. Sometimes, it involves physical activity, e.g. hitting, kicking, taking or damaging belongings. Sometimes the abuse is verbal, calling names, being insulting, teasing, or making racist or sexist remarks. Sometimes it is indirect, e.g. spreading rumours or excluding someone from social activities.

Being the victim of bullying can make life a misery. In some cases pupils can suffer physical injury. Victims of bullying are likely to be worried about attending school and this is likely to affect their concentration and learning. They will often experience anxiety-related physical symptoms and may have nightmares or attacks of anxiety. Often they will avoid attending school and try to stay at home.

Bullying occurs in all schools. A recent survey of bullying[9] found that no secondary school had fewer than 8 per cent of pupils reporting bullying.

Bullying usually occurs in and around school, in the playground, corridors, classrooms, and on the way to and from school. The most common bullies are boys or groups of boys. They tend to be involved in physical bullying. Girls tend to bully in groups and in more indirect ways, e.g. rumour, gossip. Bullying can occur in some year groups and classes more than others.

Case Study

David was a quiet and sensitive 13 year old. Since transferring to secondary school he often complained of stomach pains or headaches in the morning. Sometimes his mother allowed him to stay at home, depending on the severity of the complaint. She suspected that he was not very happy at school but assumed that it was just dislike of school work. One day he came home dishevelled, with cuts on his face and bruises on his arms. It transpired that he had been attacked by a small group from his class. After this incident, he admitted that he was being bullied and that the bullying had been going on for months. His life had been made a misery. He was laughed at, made to do humiliating things, his books were ripped, and he was called nicknames. He was afraid to tell anyone for fear of making things worse.

■ *Pupils being bullied tend not to tell teachers or their families about their difficulties.*

■ *Parents may feel uncomfortable about raising issues with teachers regarding their children's problems at school.*

Anyone can become a victim of bullying. The most vulnerable are those who are perceived as different. For instance, those who find it difficult to be assertive, those without close friends, those who behave inappropriately, and those with Special Educational Needs, particularly those with mild learning difficulties.

Racial harassment

Racial harassment is one variant of general bullying behaviour. Racism can and does occur in schools. Open racism demonstrated by staff in schools is rare but racist name calling is commonplace among pupils. Teachers vary in their responses to this. Although they often express sympathy and encourage the reporting of incidents, action is not always taken.[10,11] Where pupils retaliate for being called names, schools often apportion blame equally on both parties. This can lead some children to feel that they are being treated unfairly and ultimately they may not attend school.

Sexual harassment

Another variant of general bullying is sexual harassment. Girls are not the only victims. Boys who are homosexual or appear effeminate are particularly vulnerable. Most experience isolation and verbal abuse, many being teased, beaten up or ostracised. Often, school staff do not seem to know how to deal with the problem and therefore ignore it.[12]

Anxiety about academic performance

Current uncertainty regarding employment prospects has led to increased pressure on young people to do well in examinations. The publication of examination results to engender competition between schools has also led to increased pressure from schools and teachers. These can all lead to extreme stress, which may manifest itself in physical symptoms, e.g. headaches, viral infections, extreme tiredness, depression.

Teachers in their efforts to raise standards may also set frequent tests and extra homework. If pupils feel inadequately prepared for tests or have not completed homework they may deliberately skip that lesson to avoid getting into trouble.

In addition to general worry relating to schoolwork, some students find taking examinations extremely stressful. While coursework may seem a useful alternative to this, the pressure of meeting deadlines can also create problems. Pupils with coursework to complete may sometimes take time off school to finish it.

Anxiety can also be created where work is of an inappropriate level. When work is too difficult, fear of failure can lead to despondency and

Case Study

Laura was considered to be a promising student. She had always done well at school and her family was very supportive. When she moved into year 10 and began work specifically related to her GCSEs the pressure increased. She had more homework and coursework had to be completed to meet deadlines. Her parents constantly exhorted her to work hard so that she would do well in her GCSEs. Her teachers saw her as an able student, who might achieve Grade As in all her examinations. They gave her additional work to help her achieve this end. What was intended as encouragement was perceived by Laura as pressure. In year 11 she began to suffer from migraines. These left her unable to work and meant that she began to get behind with her work. The more she fell behind the more anxious she became and the worse her symptoms became. She began to miss a great deal of time at school. As the examinations approached things became even worse. She did manage to complete her GCSEs, but her results were well below what she was capable of achieving because of the intense anxiety she experienced.

■ *Anxiety regarding schoolwork is not confined to the less able.*

■ *Parents and teachers can unintentionally put pressure on pupils. This is likely to increase as schools and the employment market become increasingly competitive.*

subsequent apathy regarding lesson attendance. Some pupils become anxious at the prospect of failure in any guise.

Anxiety about the environment

When children transfer to a new school, particularly from a relatively small primary school to a larger secondary school, they are likely to experience some anxiety. Frequent changes of location, fear of being late or getting lost, the complexities of different lessons, fear of not having the right books, of forgetting PE kit, or other important equipment can all contribute to this anxiety.

Anxiety can also occur regarding particular aspects of the environment. Pupils often dislike using the toilet facilities at school. This may be because they are smelly, have no locks on the doors, or are used as a gathering place for others to smoke and 'mess about'. The layout of the school can provide areas where bullying can go unobserved.

Having to change and shower for PE can cause anxiety and embarrassment. It provides ideal opportunities for teasing and bullying regarding physical appearance, and interference with the belongings of others. Changing is also often characterised by extreme time pressure which some children find stressful.

Another source of anxiety can be the immediate classroom environment. For some pupils, being in a class where there are high levels of disruption can create anxiety. They may be afraid of getting into trouble and being labelled by teachers. In extreme cases they may be afraid of being physically injured.

Taking anxiety seriously

Children's anxieties and fears may seem trivial to adults. But, if we cast our minds back to our own childhoods we can probably recall the worries that we experienced then and how they affected us. They were very real. Even where children do not experience severe problems they can still be anxious on occasions. Adults should take these fears seriously.

8 Anxiety and school

Summary

- Illness is the main reason given for absence from school
- Illness can be caused by anxiety
- School circumstances can create anxiety in pupils

Anxiety about relationships can be caused by:

- Poor relations with, and fear of teachers;
- Fear of public criticism or ridicule;
- Fear of being bullied, or sexually or racially harassed;
- Fear of rejection by friends.

Anxiety related to academic performance can be caused by:

- Difficult work and fear of failure;
- Worry about poor performance in tests and examinations;
- Nervousness about taking exams;
- Pressure because of a heavy workload and the need to meet deadlines.

Anxiety related to the environment can be caused by:

- Concern regarding physical safety in some parts of the school;
- The poor behaviour of others;
- Worry about getting lost, being late, having the right equipment;
- Embarrassment about changing for PE, showering, etc.

9 Attitudes to school

This chapter focuses on factors at school that may contribute towards general apathy and alienation.

The physical environment of the school

The school environment is not always well suited to the promotion of learning or sufficiently attractive to encourage attendance. This may be through no fault of the staff. Buildings may be dilapidated, with peeling paint, inadequate lighting, heating or ventilation. Toilet facilities may be basic. There may be a lack of secure places for pupils to leave belongings and nowhere for them to congregate indoors.

Outside, playgrounds and playing fields may provide little of interest for pupils to do. Depending on school circumstances, pupils may be expected to go outside during breaks except in the most severe of weather conditions. The opportunities for bullying increase during these times, when large areas may have to be monitored, often by supervisors with limited or no training.

Split-site schools, where pupils and staff may be required to travel long distances between lessons, can disrupt the flow of learning and provide endless opportunities for pupils to 'bunk off'.

School procedures

Some children are prevented or discouraged from attending school because of school procedures. Some families may experience difficulties in providing school uniform, appropriate shoes, PE kit, or materials for practical lessons. Even where the school makes alternative provision, pupils may feel embarrassed to be different from their peers.

The cost of transport or deficiencies in its provision can also be important factors. In rural areas, where pupils rely on school buses, interruptions in services through bad weather can establish patterns of non-attendance when the service returns to normal. Disruption of train, tube or bus services in cities may have similar effects.

Older pupils may find school rules petty, particularly those relating to school uniform and general appearance. These can provide a focus for rebellion and enable pupils to legitimately not attend school because they are sent home for being inappropriately dressed.

Case Study

Tracy is 15. Her parents are divorced. When Tracy grew out of her school coat, her father bought her a denim jacket to replace it. Tracy wore the coat to go to school but was sent home by the headmistress as denim jackets were not considered suitable. Tracy's mother could not afford to buy another coat. The school provided a selection of second-hand ones for Tracy to wear but they were old. She considered them to be 'tacky' and refused to wear any of them. When it is cold she wears the denim jacket and is sent home.

- *School rules relating to uniform often seem petty to older pupils and their parents.*

- *Schools can encourage non-attendance by rigidly enforcing rules and sending pupils home.*

■ School circumstances

Circumstances within a school at particular times may also exacerbate non-attendance. Staff illness, a succession of unfamiliar supply teachers and frequent staff changes disrupt continuity in teaching and may make pupils feel demoralised. If schools have to close because of bad weather, maintenance problems, or vandalism this also disrupts the habit of attendance. Where a school is threatened with closure, low morale can have an impact on attendance.

Case Study

Observation of computerised attendance records in a secondary school over a two year period revealed that a particular year group had markedly poor overall attendance. Analysis of the reasons for this indicated that there had been problems with the school heating system in their first year which had meant unforeseen closures in a period of very bad weather. Also, at their point of entry to the school a combination of circumstances including maternity leave, staff illness and secondment had led to several changes of head of year. This meant that the problem had not been identified and tackled early on.

- *Unauthorised absenteeism can arise from combinations of unforeseen circumstances.*

- *If unauthorised absence is not identified and dealt with speedily, it is likely to become habitual.*

Attitudes to school

There has recently been great interest in pupils' attitudes towards school, including the reasons why they don't attend. On the basis of recent studies[4,5,13] it is possible to build up a picture of why some children are more motivated to attend school than others.

While the majority of pupils report being happy at school and valuing their education, relatively high numbers of pupils skip particular lessons. Pupils seem to become less satisfied as they progress through school. This is supported by the figures for non-attendance, which also increase as pupils move into years 10 and 11. In part this seems to be a reaction to school rules and discipline which are perceived as unnecessarily restrictive by older pupils, but other issues relating to the perceived purpose of school are important.

The perceived purpose of school

Generally pupils seem to have a very utilitarian view of school. They see the main function of school being to help them to:

- do well in examinations;
- acquire qualifications;
- get jobs.

Related to those they hope that they will be supported in:

- acquiring life skills, e.g. developing personal discipline, developing independence, preparing for the world;
- acquiring information and making decisions about careers, work and other options;
- doing as well as they possibly can.

Even those reporting unauthorised absence seem to share these aspirations. Many indicate that they value education and wish to continue in formal education after leaving school. They are not alienated from education itself, they simply want to miss particular classes from time to time. What reasons do they given for this?

Attitudes to teachers

The single reason most often given for missing individual lessons is that the teacher is unpleasant. This has been reported by as many as 27 per cent of non-attenders. Very few pupils report missing lessons because the teacher is unhelpful or uninterested. As pupils progress through school dislike of teachers, seems to increase.

Positively, most pupils report that teachers do mark homework and ensure that it is undertaken. But they also indicate that:

- teachers are fairly easily satisfied with standards of work;
- teachers give insufficient praise.

A minority of pupils report that teachers do not care whether they work or not.

A very large proportion of pupils report that they hardly ever or never have the opportunity to talk individually to their teachers about their schoolwork or their career plans.

Attitudes to lessons and the curriculum

When pupils are asked about lessons, approximately half report being bored in some lessons. 10 per cent report being bored in all or most lessons. Despite this 90 per cent value schoolwork and believe that it is worth doing. Only a very small minority (3 per cent) think the work they are doing is a waste of time.[13]

When the views of unauthorised absentees have been sought, the reasons they give for missing particular lessons are as follows:[4]

Unauthorised absentees' responses

The lesson is irrelevant	20%
The lesson is not enjoyable	14%
The lesson is too difficult	9%
Homework or coursework have not been completed	8%

Derived from *Truancy in English Secondary Schools: A report for the DFEE by the Truancy research project,* *1991–92,* The University of North London Truancy Unit (1994), HMSO, London.

Many pupils report missing particular lessons because they do not like the subject. The percentages of pupils reporting skipping particular lessons, because they dislike the subject is given below.

Absenteeism from lessons

PE/Games	34%
French	27%
RE	20%
Maths	19%
Science	19%
History	19%
English	18%
Technology	16%
Geography	16%

Derived from *Truancy in English Secondary Schools: A report for the DFEE by the Truancy research project,* *1991–92,* The University of North London Truancy Unit (1994), HMSO, London.

However, there may be considerable variation in this pattern between schools. In some cases it may not be particular lessons that are disliked but the way that they are taught or the way that pupils are required to work. The most favoured working activities reported[4] by pupils in years 7 and 9 are:

- working with their friends;
- making something;
- being involved in discussions.

Some pupils like working on their own, but not all. As pupils progress through school, some wish to be allowed more freedom to pursue work independently or in their own way.

Case Study

Mark is 13. He works hard at school and generally does well. The other kids refer to him as a 'boffin'. They tend to make fun of him. Physically he is of small build. He is not very good at games and doesn't like the rough and tumble of many of the activities undertaken. He also hates taking communal showers as these provide opportunities for the other boys to make fun of him. Whenever possible he avoids going to PE lessons and finds a quiet corner to get on with his work.

- *Alienation from particular lessons does not necessarily mean alienation from school in general.*

- *The curriculum or the way it is taught may lead some pupils to skip particular lessons.*

Case Study

Paul is not very good at schoolwork. He has always loved cars. He spends much of his spare time working on an old car which his older brother has bought. He wants to be a mechanic. He realises that some of his schoolwork is relevant to this ambition and works very hard in those lessons. But some subjects he sees as a waste of time. Added to that, he is not very good at them and usually is given a 'hard time' by the teachers. Sometimes he attends these lessons and messes about. At other times he just does not turn up.

- *If the curriculum is not seen by a pupil as relevant to their needs their motivation is likely to be poor.*

- *If pupils find aspects of the curriculum difficult and they are unable to engage with them, they may become disruptive.*

▰ Motivation to attend school

Positive attitudes[13] towards school tend to be associated with:

- interest in schoolwork (and lack of boredom)
- liking for teachers
- a belief in the value of school and schoolwork
- positive perceptions of the school ethos
- positive views of personal ability and perseverance
- good behaviour in school
- a high level of parental support

Schools which engender positive attitudes in their pupils tend to be seen by the pupils as having a positive ethos, a good reputation, well maintained premises, clear rules of behaviour, firm discipline, good teaching practices and high expectations. The pupils see themselves as being frequently praised and their work being marked regularly.

There is a tendency for girls to have more positive attitudes towards school than boys.

For many pupils the main reason for enjoying attending school is being with their friends[7]. This is particularly true in years 10 and 11.

Despite popular conceptions, motivation towards school and learning are only weakly associated with the type of catchment area, the type of school, the percentage of students receiving free school meals, the reading age of the intake, and GCSE results.[13]

▰ Attitudes of poor attenders

In summary disaffected pupils and those who do not attend school regularly[6,13,14] tend to:

- feel that school is a waste of time;
- dislike school;
- be uninterested in schoolwork and bored in class;
- dislike certain teachers or types of teachers;
- resent school rules;
- believe that school will not improve their career prospects;
- believe that school had done little to prepare them for life;

■ have low educational aspirations;

■ lack confidence.

For some persistent absentees school has become an alienating place. Persistent absentees, unlike those who miss particular lessons, are unlikely to stay on in full-time education. They are also more likely to be unemployed when they leave school[14]. Those living in inner-city areas tend to be more negative about school than those in other areas[6].

Attractions outside school

There is a popular view that children skip school because the activities they undertake outside are more fun or interesting. In fact, the reasons for non-attendance are many and varied. They can depend on the pupils' situation within the school, or on home or community factors, which will be discussed in Section IV. The attraction of competing activities is not usually central to abenteeism.

When children take an active decision not to attend school, they often undertake activities with friends. Students missing individual lessons often do not leave the school premises but find an isolated spot to smoke and talk, often the toilets. When taking a day off school they may spend the time sleeping, watching videos with friends, having meals at each others' houses or visiting the town.

For some pupils, at first, skipping school can be exciting. The fear of being caught and the sense of rebellion can provide great stimulation. These feelings may be enhanced by taking part in criminal activities such as shop-lifting. But, over time these sensations will cease and skipping school will become routine.

Peer pressure

The importance of peer pressure in relation to absence from school varies. This is partly because peer pressure can have a positive effect. Many pupils attend school because they want to be with their friends. Also, pupils differ in the degree to which they will conform to pressure from others. However, where non-attendance has become the norm within a peer group, there will be greater pressure to conform. This is particularly true of areas where there is general alienation[14]. This will be discussed more fully in Chapter 13.

Sometimes pupils feel that they have outgrown school. If they have a job and older friends who are already working, their company may be more attractive.

Case Study

Tracy is 15. She had a good attendance record at school until year 9. She wanted to be a hairdresser and was anticipating going to college when she left school. In year 9 her attendance at school began to deteriorate. When the school contacted her parents it became clear that they too were concerned. She had an older boyfriend and was constantly in his company. All attempts by her parents to get her to go to school regularly or see less of this boy had met with failure.

- *Some adolescents may develop social relationships which shift their focus away from school-related matters.*

- *Parents can sometimes be powerless to make their children attend school.*

Child employment

There has been a recent increase in the number of school pupils undertaking paid employment. Britain has the largest child workforce in Europe accounting for one third of Europe's working children. Up to a million of these children are employed illegally, either because they are too young for the jobs they are doing or because they are working illegal hours.

The law governing child employment is based on the Children and Young Persons Act of 1933. This forbids the employment of any child under 13, and limits the hours children over 13 and under 16 can work to two hours a day. Children may also work for four hours on Saturday or 8 hours if they are over 15. The working week may not exceed 20 hours for under 15s, or 30 hours for 16 year olds still at school. However, local authorities have the power to modify these requirements through bylaws. This means that there is wide local variation. Some employment is not regulated at all.

The type of employment undertaken by school pupils is varied. Common are paper rounds, milk rounds, shop and restaurant work, working in markets and at car boot sales, pizza delivery on bikes, agricultural work, child care, and babysitting.

The motives for undertaking paid employment are mixed. In some cases pupils wish to have extra spending money,[15] in others they may be supplementing the family's income. They may also enjoy the responsibility and the adult status conferred upon them when they are working. For these reasons working for a few hours each week can have beneficial effects. However, once the level exceeds 10 hours each week,[16] education is adversely affected.

Case Study

Cliff is 14. His father has retired from work because of ill health and his mother is unemployed. He has two brothers younger than himself. He works on a milk round during the week. He gets up at four in the morning and as a result of this often falls asleep in lessons. Sometimes he is late for school and some days he is too tired to attend at all. His homework is rarely completed and his schoolwork has deteriorated since he took the job. But he is aware that the money he earns is vital to supplement the family income and this makes him feel very proud and responsible.

■ *While pupils who are persistently late or absent from school may be perceived by the school as irresponsible, their reasons may be morally irreprehensible.*

Undertaking paid employment may contribute to non-attendance directly, when the child misses school to go to work, and indirectly when the child may miss school because of tiredness, uncompleted homework or coursework. There is no doubt that long hours spent working have a bad effect on education.[17] Examination results, attendance and commitment to continuing education have all been shown to be affected.

9 Attitudes to School

Summary

Aspects of the school affecting attendance:

* physical environment;
* procedures;
* circumstances.

Pupils tend to have a utilitarian view of school. They see it as a means to:

* gain qualifications;
* prepare for the world of work;
* acquire life skills;
* socialise with their friends.

If school does not satisfy these needs, pupils may become alienated.

Attractions outside school are not usually sufficiently great on their own to lead to non-attendance, although social relationships and work responsibilities can be important influences.

10 Making school more attractive

Schools which achieve high levels of attendance have adopted policies which 'incorporate' pupils and their families, encouraging them to participate in school life. Interpersonal rather than impersonal relationships are established and good behaviour is rewarded in preference to bad behaviour being punished.

This positive, inclusive ethos contrasts with those schools with lower levels of attendance, where a coercive approach has been adopted. High levels of punishment are in evidence, with high levels of institutional control. There are many detailed school rules, which are interpreted strictly. Such schools have a low level of tolerance of any kind of individuality and are also characterised by providing little or no support for parents.

Developing a school ethos which encourages good attendance requires the establishment of an environment which is attractive and supportive for pupils, staff and parents. Three important aspects can be identified, although there is considerable overlap between them:

- the physical environment;
- the social climate;
- the learning and working environment.

The physical environment

The first thing which any visitor to a school will notice is the physical environment. Peeling paint, dirt, litter, graffiti, etc. will not create a favourable impression. For those working in the school the initial impact will soon fade, but if the physical environment is characterised by neglect this will inevitably pervade the attitudes of staff and pupils, making it difficult for them to take a pride in the school.

Involving pupils in creating an attractive physical environment is vital if you wish them to respect it. If they take part in the decision-making process and are involved in its implementation, vandalism is much less likely to occur. The first step in this process involves consultation with the pupils, to establish the facilities they would like to be available in school. Different groups of pupils will have different requirements. A means of prioritising these, which is seen to be fair, will need to be devised.

Staff, similarly, will have ideas about the nature of the school environment and how it can be improved. The priorities of staff and pupils may not be the same and sensitive planning and negotiation is likely to be required to ensure that everyone feels that their views have been taken into account. If the planning is seen in the long, rather than short term, this should be possible.

Major projects

Making major changes to the physical environment of the school can be constrained by financial considerations. However, smaller projects are often possible with the assistance of pupils, staff, and parents. Local businesses may also be willing to make contributions, either financially, or by providing materials. Such projects have the added advantage of increasing feelings of ownership and commitment to the school.

Some projects may not require major structural changes but a reallocation of room usage, decoration and the provision of appropriate furniture. Some developments which schools have found useful specifically in relation to attendance issues are outlined below:

- a pleasantly decorated parents' room;
- a quiet study room;
- a quiet room away from the public eye, where pupils can meet with professionals from outside the school, e.g. EWOs, Educational Psychologists;
- an indoor games room;
- social areas for each year group;
- a designated girls only room;
- improved toilet facilities;
- a place of safe storage for pupils' belongings.

▬ Access

In the effort to improve links with parents and the wider school community, access to the school is very important.

Particularly crucial in this respect is signposting. From personal experience, over many years, I know that schools often do not provide adequate signposting. For parents visiting the school this can be very daunting. Clear signposting to the reception area and instructions for what to do when you get there, e.g. please knock and enter, ring bell, etc. are essential. Creating a friendly, informal atmosphere is also important if the school genuinely wishes to make parents feel welcome. Providing comfortable chairs where visitors can sit and wait with something to look at, e.g. displays of pupils' work, magazines, information about the school, creates an appropriate atmosphere. Other important considerations are:

- access for the disabled;
- adequately signposted and labelled toilet facilities;
- car parking.

▬ The school grounds

The immediate outdoor environment of the school can provide places where pupils skipping lessons can go to avoid detection, and be the site of bullying incidents. It is also vulnerable to vandalism.

Recently, many schools have taken measures to improve their grounds. They have attempted to create an environment which is safe, secure, interesting, flexible and easy to supervise. Areas where pupils may undertake differing activities have been established, e.g. for playing football, sitting and talking. Focal points have been created where pupils can meet. Areas where bullying may occur or truants may congregate have been identified and are regularly patrolled by staff. Security has been increased to prevent vandalism and theft, for instance by improving boundary fencing and surveillance and reducing the number of places of access. This also assists in the monitoring of pupils leaving the premises during school time without permission.

Similar procedures to those described in Chapter 4 can be adopted to establish the needs and wishes of pupils and staff in relation to the external environment of the school, e.g. questionnaires, discussions, establishing the good and bad features of the existing environment, brainstorming sessions. Pupils can also draw maps of the school and its surroundings and mark in the activities they undertake in different places. Useful information to be collected includes:

- how outdoor facilities are currently used;
- areas where bullying occurs;
- the kinds of sporting activities that pupils would like to be able to undertake outside;
- other facilities that students would like outdoors;
- the effectiveness of supervision outdoors.

When the information has been collated and priorities are to be established, it is important to ensure that consideration has been given to:

- vehicular access;
- access between buildings;
- litter bins;
- access to cloakrooms and toilet facilities;
- seating.

Maintenance and cleanliness

The general maintenance and cleanliness of the school is important for health and safety reasons in addition to its role in sustaining the morale of staff and pupils. Lighting, heating and appropriate ventilation are particularly important. It is difficult to work if conditions are either extremely hot or cold, or where there is a lack of fresh air. Poor or badly-maintained lighting, e.g. flickering fluorescent lights, can damage eyesight and/or give rise to headaches.

Cleanliness in the school is also important. Litter and graffiti create an impression of neglect. Dirty classrooms, corridors and toilets convey a message to staff and pupils that their learning and working environment is not valued.

Decoration

Although pupils and teachers may have limited control over many aspects of their physical environment, they can take responsibility for displays and decoration around the school. To reduce internal vandalism, pupils should be involved as much as possible and be given sole responsibility for some displays. For instance, notice boards in tutorial rooms can be made the responsibility of the pupils in that tutor group.

In addition to the traditional displays of artwork, projects, etc., photographs of pupils taking part in school trips, plays, musical activities, work experience, and classroom activities can be used. Displays can also convey information about forthcoming events, attendance levels, parents' evenings and so on.

▓ The social climate

The social climate of the school is critical in engendering a suitable environment for learning. If children are afraid of being bullied, and there is constant disruption both in and out of lessons, the possibility of effective learning taking place will be considerably reduced. Some quotations from recent work[18] on learning in the secondary school illustrate how pupils can be affected by an adverse social climate.

'Like last year one of the fifth years came bullying me and I ended up with a black eye because he wopped me around the head with his bag . . . . I didn't want to come to school because I was scared' (Year 8 pupil, male).

'... like Ms X: Sometimes when I were a first year, she prodded me and I went flying, and sometimes she swears a bit as well' (Year 8 pupil, male).

The reduction of incidents of bullying and the improvement of the social climate of the school depends on mutual respect. OFSTED[19] recommend that school behaviour policies should include as one of their aims, the encouragement of self discipline in pupils. This requires that schools try to encourage greater openness in classrooms, promote good teacher-pupil–relationships, engender high self-esteem in pupils and create the kind of social and learning environment in which pupils will wish to participate.

Bringing about this kind of change requires a similar level of commitment as that required to improve school attendance. The school needs to develop a code of behaviour which outlines the responsibilities of pupils and staff and implement it, effectively. It is beyond the scope of this book to explore these issues in sufficient depth. Further reading and sources of information are given in Section VI. However, an example of a bill of rights, derived from Brownhills High School, Staffordshire, is given opposite.

Rights and responsibilities

1. We have the right to be treated with respect by all people irrespective of age, gender, colour or status.
   We have the responsibility to respect all others within our community.
2. We have the right to an education and to learn according to our ability.
   We have the responsibility not to ridicule others for the way in which they learn, or to disturb the learning of others.
3. We have the right to feel safe in and around the school.
   We have the responsibility to ensure the safety of all pupils by behaving in a reasonable manner in and around school.
4. We have the right not to be bullied in any way, shape or form.
   We have the responsibility not to bully others and to report any bullying we see.
5. We have the right to express our own opinions and to be heard.
   We have the responsibility to allow others to express their opinions and to be heard.
6. We have the right to choose our friends.
   We have the responsibility not to force our friendship upon others or to abuse the friendship.
7. We have the right to play in safety and without interference.
   We have the responsibility not to disrupt, or endanger, the play of others.
8. We have the right to expect that our possessions will be secure in and around school.
   We have the responsibility not to steal or mistreat the possessions of others and to report any theft or mistreatment that we see.

Derived from a policy developed by Brownhills High School, Staffordshire.

Code of behaviour

Once the process of developing a code of behaviour has been undertaken and the code is established, the school needs to ensure that it is put into practice. This will be assisted by:

- Staff in leadership roles within the school demonstrating behaviour commensurate with the code, thereby providing examples of appropriate behaviour;
- Staff at all levels demonstrating appropriate behaviour, thereby providing positive examples for pupils;
- Firm and fair action being taken where there is evidence of inappropriate behaviour from pupils or staff;
- An emphasis on the positive aspects of the behaviour and work of staff and pupils. Criticism, where necessary being constructive;
- Praise, positive approval, concrete rewards being given for good behaviour;
- Setting up school councils to allow pupils to influence decision making;
- Providing systems in the school where pupils can get help and advice;
- Ensuring that pupils know how to access such systems;
- Ensuring that levels of stress are appropriate for staff and pupils. Too little can result in boredom and lack of interest; too much can lead to anxiety and defensive aggressive behaviour.

Teacher–pupil relationships

The quality of teacher–pupil relationships is central to creating a positive social climate. Not all pupils and teachers relate easily to one another. Schools need to ensure that there are minimum standards of behaviour on both sides.

As we saw earlier, dislike of particular teachers is the major cause of post-registration truancy. To encourage pupils to attend their lessons regularly, teachers need to treat pupils with respect, whatever their personal feelings towards them.

Traditionally, schools have tended not to adopt such an ethos. Historically, the relationships between teachers and pupils have been determined by the power structures operating in the school. Such systems do not sit well with the current emphasis on children's rights. But as pupils from recent research[18] indicate, the most positive relationships between teachers and pupils are founded on such respect:

'. . . the nicest teachers ... treat you like you should be treated, not like a child or unimportant' (year 8 pupil, female).

'. . . some teachers are OK, like they treat you with the same respect as they would with – well, nearly the same respect as they would with an adult ...' (year 8 pupils, female).

The development and implementation of a behaviour policy will go some way towards addressing these issues. Where teachers experience difficulties operating within such a framework the school will need to take action. Such cases can be extremely problematic and will need appropriate support systems for staff within the school.

Accommodating changing pupil needs

As pupils progress through school, their needs, in relation to learning and the social environment, change.[18] In year 7, the excitement and anxiety of starting a new school tend to overshadow everything else. The school functions as a social centre, and the complexities of the pupils' social worlds leads to a preoccupation with things other than learning. In year 8, school life becomes more routine and students want to be treated more as adults. In years 9, 10 and 11, as external examinations approach, the emphasis changes to a greater concern with learning.

If schools take account of the differences in pupils' social needs as they become older, attendance is less likely to decline in years 10 and 11.

For younger pupils it is important to:

- ensure that playgrounds are safe environments;
- stagger lunchtimes to minimise contact and possible friction between young and older pupils;
- ensure that ancillary staff on duty at lunchtime have appropriate training.

Older pupils benefit from:

- An acceptance that they need time and space for themselves and the facilities to make this possible;
- The setting up of youth clubs in lunch breaks;
- Being allowed to set up their own social activities;
- Evening social activities, where youth workers are available for young people to discuss things that they might find difficult to share with teachers;
- Being given some responsibility for the monitoring of behaviour.

The social life of the school as a whole may benefit from:

- providing access to sports facilities, the library, and social areas during break times;

- encouraging students to become involved in after school activities, e.g. sports, music, cooking, gardening;
- making arrangements for the school to provide breakfast.

The learning and working environment

Pupils spend the majority of their time at school in the classroom. It is therefore crucial that the learning environment is conducive to working.

In year 7 pupils are preoccupied with adjustment to their new school and learning in itself is not a central consideration. In some schools, at the end of this year, pupils are streamed or put into sets. For some this can mark the beginning of the establishment of a negative learning image. If setting or streaming is to occur, staff need to be aware of the feelings of failure that this can engender and the possible impact on pupil motivation. Sensitivity will be required from teachers to reassure pupils that they can succeed at school and that they have a valuable contribution to make to society.

In year 9, motivation may be increased by the prospect of choosing options. For some, outings and activities outside school can become more motivating than routine schoolwork. At this point students who have missed school may begin to realise that they have gaps in their learning. Schools can respond positively to this by providing opportunities for additional support. This may be in relation to basic skills, substantive curriculum work or study skills.

In years 10 and 11 pupils sense the change of pace and begin to feel the pressure of forthcoming examinations. The importance of this cannot be underestimated. Homework becomes more important, coursework has to be completed on time and revision strategies have to be developed. The higher the career aspirations of the pupil the greater the pressure.

Work experience can also be important, highlighting the need for examination success to achieve career aspirations and increasing motivation. For those not taking examinations, however, this can mark the start of a downward decline where the purpose of attending school becomes meaningless.

Motivation in the classroom

Unsuccessful classroom practices are those which discourage students from becoming involved with their work. Motivating pupils is one of

Engaging classrooms

In what ways can classrooms encourage a positive style of learning motivation?

Tasks

- Design activities that make learning interesting and that involve variety and personal challenge;
- Help learners establish realistic goals. With short-term goals, students view their class-work as manageable, and they can focus on their progress and what they are learning;
- Help students develop organizational and management skills and effective task strategies. Students, especially those with learning difficulties, need to develop and apply strategies for planning, organizing and monitoring their work.

Authority

- Give students opportunities to participate actively in the learning process via leadership roles, choices and decision-making;
- Help students develop the skills that will enable them to take responsibility for their learning.

Recognition

- Recognize individual student effort, accomplishments and improvement;
- Give all students opportunities to receive reward and recognition;
- Give recognition and rewards privately so that their value is not derived at the expense of others.

Grouping

- Provide opportunities for cooperative group learning and peer interaction;
- Use heterogeneous and varied grouping arrangements.

Evaluation

- Evaluate students for individual progress, improvement and mastery;
- Give students opportunities to improve their performance;
- Vary the method of evaluation and make evaluation private.

Time

- Adjust task or time requirements for students who have difficulty completing their work;
- Allow students opportunities to plan their schedules and progress at an optimal rate.

Derived from the work of Ames[20] and Epstein[21]

the most vital tasks of a teacher. It is particularly important if pupils are to be persuaded to attend school regularly. While it is beyond the scope of this book to cover these issues in depth, a clear summary of the ways that teachers can provide engaging classrooms is provided by the 'TARGET' acronym.[20,21] This is presented in the box on page 129.

Implicit in this formulation is the assumption that teachers will have high expectations of all their pupils. Helping staff achieve these aims may require the provision of staff training. Further reading and sources of information regarding the development of motivation in the classroom are given in Section VI.

▨ The curriculum

The curriculum itself can have a motivating or demotivating effect. Some pupils 'bunk off' because they dislike particular lessons. Although, the National Curriculum exerts considerable constraints on the freedom of schools to develop their own curriculum, they do have freedom to develop the means of delivery of the curriculum. This is crucial to student motivation. Pupils report that they dislike completing work sheets and copying from the board, but enjoy working in groups and participating in activities outside school. Teachers need to be creative in their presentation of materials, adopting different techniques and providing a stimulating and varied programme of work if they are to engage pupils in learning.

If pupils make inappropriate option choices in year 9, this can have a devastating effect on their motivation and subsequent attendance. To prevent this, appropriate guidance regarding option choices needs to be provided. When pupils begin options, subject teachers should undertake regular assessment of academic progress to detect difficulties. Depending on the nature of these, learning support may be provided or options can be changed. Schools need a clear and flexible policy on changing options.

▨ Basic skills

There is a strong link between poor attendance and poor literacy. If pupils have insufficient basic skills then they may be unable to fully participate in what is going on in their lessons. Lessons will then be perceived as 'boring'.

A number of LEAs and schools have successfully provided additional classes for improving literacy. These have proved extremely popular with pupils. Attendance has been good and pupils' basic skills have shown considerable improvement. Such intervention is likely to be particularly successful if undertaken early in a pupil's school career, before non-attendance becomes a serious problem. Some schools have also found it beneficial to provide learning support classes before and after school and in the lunch hour. Homework clubs where a teacher is available to provide assistance if it is required have also proved popular.

Learning support provided in curriculum lessons can also be effective.

Examination entry

Exam entry policies have an important impact on attendance. Pupils tend to have a utilitarian approach to their education. They see it as preparing them for work, mainly through gaining qualifications. If they are not entered for GCSE examinations they may see little point in attending school in the latter part of year 11, when schoolwork is largely oriented to exam preparation. To ensure a wider examination entry, schools can explore alternative examination options. A range of vocational qualifications and examinations in basic skills are now available. Where schools have provided opportunities for students to take these, motivation and attendance have improved.

Study skills

As pupils progress through school and become aware of the importance of doing well in coursework and examinations, many report a lack of study skills. Teachers exhort them to work harder but this has little meaning. They do not know how to go about organising their time, making their learning more effective or revising for examinations. Schools can help by setting up study skills courses. These might address issues relating to:

- time management;
- planning work;
- setting up a suitable learning environment at home;
- note-taking techniques;
- accessing information;
- presentation of work;
- word processing skills.

Examination skills and stress

Many pupils experience examination stress. In some cases this can be severe. Schools can support pupils by providing short courses which consider revision strategies, examination techniques, and also introduce coping strategies for examination nerves.

Catching up on work

If pupils miss school for any reason they may have problems in catching up with work. Once a pupil has fallen behind, subsequent lessons may be difficult to comprehend and motivation may deteriorate. The teacher can also experience frustration at having to try to support someone who is unable to work with the rest of the class because of missed lessons. In this situation, the pupil can become demoralised and begin to deliberately skip lessons.

Schools can help by providing support for catching up, either in lessons, with a support teacher, or during non-lesson time, e.g. at lunch time. The development of curriculum materials which can be used for independent work is also useful. Pupils need to be given reasonable deadlines for the completion of work. To avoid adverse effects on motivation the help should be provided immediately, before the problem escalates. The subject teacher has the responsibility for identifying problems quickly and requesting additional support for the pupil, where necessary.

Work experience

Many schools provide opportunities for pupils to gain work experience. This is valuable for all pupils. Where pupils' strengths do not lie in academic work, carefully selected placements, which reflect pupils' interests, can be particularly important in motivating them to work hard at school and to gain the necessary qualifications and skills. In the case of students who are persistent truants or who are at risk of exclusion some schools have extended this provision. This will be considered in Section V in relation to working with individuals.

Compact schemes

Compact schemes develop the curriculum through links with industry and commerce. These can also improve motivation. A mentor, who is an employee in the company, works with the pupil. Each participating pupil has a contract and a set of aims devised jointly by themselves and their mentor. These include regular attendance at school and punctuality. Such schemes have proved extremely successful in motivating pupils to greater effort at school.

Individual tutorial support

Pupils feel more valued and attach more importance to feedback when they are given individual attention. This is particularly important in relation to progress at school and consultations relating to option choices and careers. Schools need to provide regular opportunities for students to meet individually with their form tutors and discuss issues relating to school which are important to them. This has resource implications relating to the time of form tutors.

What a good school should be like

In considering the question of making school more attractive, attention has been drawn to the physical environment, the social environment and the learning environment. Each has been considered separately but there is considerable overlap between them. It is the 'whole-school' climate which is important.

Peers School in Oxford produced a description of a good school as a result of a brainstorming session by teachers and pupils. The document demonstrates the way that staff and pupils can identify and work towards a view of how they would like their school to be.

Staff development

The implications for staff training in relation to the whole-school approach to promoting good attendance are enormous. Training requirements may be very diverse. Schools need to be aware that teaching and non-teaching staff may require training and be prepared to take these requirements seriously. Arranging joint sessions may in some cases be beneficial, reinforcing the idea that everyone, whatever their position, is working towards similar ends. Staff may particularly benefit from training relating to:

- lunchtime supervision;
- anti-bullying procedures;
- the promotion of positive behaviour;
- techniques for conflict resolution and diffusing difficult situations;
- interpersonal skills training;
- equal opportunities.

What should a 'good' school have?

a) A feeling of community

- Good relationships
- Happy people
- Not being afraid
- Students not picked on by staff – No bullying
- Talking openly and honestly

b) A positive atmosphere

- Lots of praise for achievement, academic and non-academic
- Everyone making progress
- Exciting, not boring
- Relevant, interesting

c) A broad view of education

- Being concerned with more than the National Curriculum
- Continuing education
- Contact after leaving school
- Extra curricular activities

d) An attractive environment

- Respect for the environment and buildings

e) A sense of purpose

- People should be punctual
- The school should be efficient

f) A self-critical stance

- Openness to change
- Be self critical

Peers Community School, Oxford.

Effecting change in the learning environment may require teaching staff to undertake training in relation to:

- classroom management;
- differentiation;
- using multi-media teaching techniques;
- motivating students;
- teaching basic skills;
- teaching study skills and examination techniques;
- the operation of compact schemes.

To achieve lasting improvements in school attendance, fundamental changes in school environment, physical, social and working, may need to be made.

---

10 Making school more attractive

Summary

Schools are places for work. As such they need to provide:

- A safe, pleasant physical environment;
- A safe and warm social climate;
- Conditions conducive to learning and work.

These can most effectively be achieved by:

- Establishing and providing for the needs of the pupils and staff;
- Encouraging staff and student participation in decision making, and the implementation and monitoring of changes;
- Developing and actively implementing a code of conduct for pupils and staff;
- Promoting work-oriented attitudes in classrooms;
- Providing opportunities for staff development.

SECTION IV
FACTORS OUTSIDE
SCHOOL AFFECTING
ATTENDANCE

11 The family

The influence of the family in relation to attendance and performance at school cannot be underestimated. Families can have a positive or negative influence. The circumstances in which families find themselves can affect a child's education.

Even illness can be viewed in different ways by different families. Some parents will send their children to school when they may be quite ill, while others will keep children at home for minor illnesses. An important factor may be whether there is anyone available to look after the child at home. A recent survey,[22] suggests that the children of mothers with full-time jobs miss less schooling through sickness than pupils whose mothers do not go to work. Working mothers seem more likely to send their children to school when they have a minor illness.

The positive influence of the family

When a child does not attend school regularly, there is a tendency for the child's parents to be blamed. Although family circumstances can contribute towards absenteeism families can also contribute to its reduction. A recent survey[4] revealed that 48 per cent of pupils did not truant because they were afraid of their parents finding out. Parental support and interest are important in explaining the attitudes of pupils towards school.[13]

Parents generally have very positive attitudes towards their child's school:[15]

- most would recommend the school that their child is attending;
- think the school is either good or very good;
- believe that their children are well cared for;

- think that teachers are approachable and treat them as partners in their child's education;
- feel very welcome in the school.

Only a small minority express concern about examination results in their child's school. Most would like more information, particularly about extra-curricula activities and what their children are learning. Generally they are keen to help their children but lack confidence in their ability to do so. Such positive support for schools from parents suggests that most are unlikely to condone unauthorised absence.

■ Family pressures

Most parents are unaware of their child's absenteeism. Some, who are aware of it, feel powerless to prevent it. There are others who require their children to be at home to help out either financially or in caring for other members of the family to the detriment of school attendance.

Twenty per cent of children[23] are currently being brought up in single parent families and it is likely that the pressures on them are greater.

Case Study

Jane is 11. She enjoys going to school, her work is good and she has a lot of friends. Her parents are divorced. She lives with her mother and two younger brothers. Her mother works as a secretary in a large company. Jane regularly helps her mother in the house. Sometimes, if her brothers are unwell and need to stay away from school, Jane will take time off school to look after them. Her mother feels guilty about this, but there have been a lot of redundancies in the company recently and she is afraid that if she takes time off work she will lose her job. This would create very difficult financial circumstances for the family.

- *Parents may sometimes have to make difficult choices between their child attending school and other urgent family needs.*

- *Children may wish to attend school but have little choice when they have family responsibilities.*

▨ Young carers

Estimates suggest that there are 10,000 children nationally who have primary caring responsibilities.[24,25] This may involve caring for parents who have profound physical disabilities, who are terminally ill, or who have psychiatric problems. The impact of caring in relation to a child's education can be profound. In addition to carrying out household tasks they often have to undertake personal tasks for their parent, e.g. washing, dressing, assisting in bathing. Leaving their parents at home while they go to school can cause anxiety and often they do not go. When they do attend, they may be late, not have completed homework, and be suffering from emotional stress and tiredness having looked after the adult at night. They may be afraid to share their problems with staff, because they fear that the person who is ill might be taken away, or with peers, because they do not wish to appear different. This can be particularly acute when the parent has psychiatric problems.

Case Study

Diane is 15 and an only child. Her mother has Multiple Sclerosis. She has been caring for her since she was 8 years old, when her father left home. She undertakes all of the domestic tasks at home and some personal caring for her mother. She tries to attend school, but when her mother's condition deteriorates or her mother is ill in addition to the Multiple Sclerosis, this is impossible. The school is aware of the mother's condition and has been supportive in trying to help her attend parents' evenings. But the staff seem to have no conception of the day-to-day problems which Diane experiences. Support in relation to schoolwork has not been forthcoming; incomplete homework is met with a negative rather than a sympathetic response; absence from school is not commented upon. Diane has no one at school to whom she can turn to even discuss the problems she faces.

■ *While schools and individual teachers may be sympathetic to children with difficulties at home, school structures and systems are not always sufficiently flexible to enable teachers to give additional help, without creating undue stress on time. Current financial stringency can exacerbate this problem.*

The children of travellers

Travelling communities have no history or tradition of formal education. Historically, their children have been educated by their families within their community. In recognition of their way of life, traveller parents are protected from conviction regarding their children's school attendance providing that the children attend school for a minimum of 200 half days each year. If travellers are living on legal sites, or in houses, for part of the year, their children may be able to attend one school, with authorised absence being granted for planned periods of travel, where the school expects that the family will return. In these cases children can be provided with distance learning materials for periods of travel and be given additional support when they are at school.

Particular problems arise when families living on illegal sites are evicted, having to move on. This can disrupt the child's education. Constantly moving can mean that there are insufficient school places for children moving into particular catchment areas. Schools may also be reluctant to accept children who are late starters or who have intermittent learning experiences. Traveller children can also be victims of prejudice and discrimination and may experience difficulties in adjusting to institutional life which is unfamiliar to them.

Poverty

According to European Union figures, 20 per cent of the UK population are now experiencing poverty. The number of children living in families dependent on benefits has doubled in the last ten years. The value of supplementary benefit/income support as a proportion of full-time male earnings fell from 26 per cent to 19 per cent. Approximately 20 per cent of children are being brought up in single parent families. These factors are likely to influence children's behaviour and performance in school. The links between poverty, ill-health and educational under-achievement are well documented.[23] Poverty can mean that children may not be able to afford proper school uniform, materials for lessons, and other essential equipment. If may also mean that pupils take part-time jobs to supplement the income of their family. All of these factors have an impact upon pupils' attendance at school.

Unemployment

Unemployment in the family can have further effects. Studies in Europe[26] indicate that children with unemployed fathers perform less well in school and in some cases a decline in performance has been traced directly to the time when the father became unemployed,[27] Attendance can also be affected. Where parents are unemployed, particularly for long periods of time, the routine pattern of work is broken. School pupils may be left to get themselves ready for school, while others stay in bed. Unemployment can also put a strain on relationships, where family members are at home together all day.

Homelessness

Approximately half-a-million children were affected by homelessness in the 1980s. Living in temporary accommodation disrupts schooling and adversely affects performance.[28] Problems of overcrowding in bed and breakfast accommodation create immense problems, particularly with homework. Many of the homeless are from ethnic minorities; some are refugees. Living in temporary accommodation means that they may have to make frequent and sudden moves. Attendance at school can therefore be irregular. Some pupils do not enroll at all. Others may have to wait for a place. All this contributes to disruption in schooling and may establish a pattern of non-attendance.

Severe family stress

Some children will experience extremely difficult home circumstances. Home life may be characterised by:

- Alcoholism
- Drug abuse
- Sexual abuse
- Violence
- Unstable adult relationships
- Difficult relationships between adults and children
- An uncaring environment

Coping with severe family stress may place such demands on the child that school is seen as relatively unimportant in their lives. Even for children where stress is not severe there may be a conflict of interests between a perceived need to be at home and the desire to go to school. Schools have an important role in providing a stable, caring and supportive environment which may assist children in coping with family difficulties.

Case Study

John is 10. His mother suffers from periods of alcoholism. His father has recently left home after years of abusive and violent behaviour towards John, his younger brother, and their mother. John likes school, enjoys the company of other children, tries hard with his work and is progressing steadily. However, he is often away from school because he is afraid to leave his mother and younger brother at home alone. He worries that his mother may have an accident during a drinking bout, may set fire to the house by leaving a cigarette alight or that his father may return and the violence recommence. For the same reason he is often afraid to go to sleep at night.

▪ *Children may feel that their fears and responsibilities at home are more pressing than their schooling.*

▪ *Schools, collaborating with other services, can provide stability and support in such cases.*

Children who are 'looked after' by local authorities

For some extremely vulnerable children, there is a clear role for other agencies to support the family. In some cases, if the court is satisfied that they are 'suffering, or at risk of significant harm', a child may be made the subject of a care order. Since the implementation of the Children Act (1989), care orders and court action for child protection have shown a significant fall. Where orders are granted they are generally shorter. Parents, while they may in the short term be denied access to their child, retain their legal relationship. It is now extremely rare for a care order to be made solely in relation to poor attendance at school.

Whatever the reasons for a care order, being removed from their family, even within this changed framework, can have considerable effects on children. Their behaviour is likely to be affected. They may feel rejected, and therefore react badly to criticism. They often have little interest in school and there is considerable evidence that children who are 'looked after' by local authorities carry a high risk of educational failure.[29] A report by OFSTED and the Department of Health[30] showed that a high percentage of these children at Key Stage 4 had a history of poor attendance or were excluded from schools and did not have regular contact with education. Generally, in provision for their care, educational progress and standards were not given equal footing with such matters as relationships and contact with parents.

███ The importance of families

Children only spend six or seven hours of each weekday at school. Much of their time is spent with their families. It is unrealistic for schools to ignore family influences. For some children the demands or trauma of family life can be so great that the impact on their attendance and behaviour at school is profound. Schools have a vital role to play in such circumstances, providing a stable and supportive environment for the child.

11 The family

Summary

- Children spend a relatively small proportion of their lives at school
- Families have an enormous influence on their children's lives
- Most families are supportive of their children attending school
- Where families experience problems these will inevitably affect their children's behaviour and performance at school
- Where problems are very severe they may overshadow all other aspects of the child's life
- Schools can play a key role in supporting children whose families are experiencing problems.

12 Home–school links

Schools have shared interests with parents in promoting pupils' attendance at school and their achievement when they are there.

Ensuring that their children attend school is legally the responsibility of parents. Once at school, for most parents, their initial concern is that their child will be safe and happy. Concerns about academic achievement almost always take a secondary place to this, although most parents are anxious that their child does as well as they can. To this end, most provide support for their child, to the extent that they feel they can.

Since the advent of league tables, schools have had a particular interest in raising overall levels of attainment. To satisfy this aim, schools must raise the standards of all pupils. To achieve this, every child must be encouraged to attend school regularly and work hard. These concerns are shared with parents. To develop home–school partnerships, which support children in their education, is in the best interests of all concerned. Schools should therefore encourage closer links with parents.

A first step in this process can be to establish what parents want from the school. To ascertain the needs and wishes of the parents of the children attending your school, it is relatively simple to undertake a survey. The fact that you are canvassing parental views will in itself be a major step towards promoting better home–school links.

When schools have undertaken such surveys, the responses have generally indicated that parents want more information. The box below outlines the responses made by one group of parents to a questionnaire sent out by a school.

What do parents want?

Responses to a questionnaire asking parents what they wanted from school. Parents requested:

1. Better communication about their child's progress and behaviour and any subsequent action to be taken by the school

2. To be informed at an early stage if there are concerns regarding their child's attendance or ability to learn in a mainstream setting

3. Better careers' advice for their children

4. Counselling to be available

5. To be able to approach teachers without feeling intimidated

6. All detentions to take place during school hours

7. Parents' groups to be set up to deal with particular issues, e.g. truanting, bullying and behaviour problems

8. Contact addresses of education support systems, e.g. Educational Psychologists, Education Welfare Officers, etc.

Keeping parents informed

Parents need to be provided with up-to-date information regarding general developments in the school. They also require detailed information about their own child's progress. Communication can be made in a number of ways.

School booklet

This should provide basic information about the school and contain clear statements of the schools' expectations on a number of matters pertaining to school, e.g. dress, attendance, punctuality, homework, school rules, etc.

Newsletters

These are usually written in an informal style and provide parents with information about current events at school, special projects, pupils' achievements, school trips and issues of general interest. Information of crucial importance would not normally be included.

Letters home

These can provide information of a general nature or related to a specific child. They are particularly relevant when there have been changes in school rules, particular problems in some area of school life, or to communicate important information about forthcoming events in the child's school life, e.g. work experience, examinations. If the information is of critical importance, schools would be well advised to provide a tear-off slip for parents to return, confirming that they have received the information. This is useful to encourage parents to attend parents' evenings, joint PTAs, become school governors, etc.

To get the message across effectively letters should be:

- direct;
- easy to read;
- short;
- translated into the languages used in the school community;
- illustrated with graphics.

Parents also require information about their own child. This may be a report on progress and particular achievement, or to express concern. Traditionally, reports on pupils' progress have been sent out in a 'school report' at the end of the term, or delivered at formal parents' evenings. Recently, schools have found an increase in pupil motivation when letters praising attendance, behaviour or achievement have been sent home during the course of the term. Where there are concerns about a child's progress, parents also prefer to be informed of the situation early so that they can provide support for their child. Guided by the school, parents are often able to provide a level of individual attention, impossible in the school setting, which may prove beneficial in helping a child overcome learning difficulties.

Telephone communication

This is invaluable for following up absence speedily. If a school has received no communication from parents on the first day of absence, when this is the normal procedure, the school can make contact by telephone. It may also be useful in making contact, when a dialogue is required with parents about their child and they are unable to attend the school.

Welcoming parents into school

Some parents find schools very threatening places. This may be in part because of their own experiences at school. If schools genuinely want to improve links with parents then they must recognise parents' fears and attempt to overcome them. An initial step is to create a welcoming environment (see Chapter 10).

Parents can also be encouraged to take a more active part in the life of the school. Setting up PTAs can give parents the opportunity to help in a practical way. Encouraging parents to take responsibilities as parent governors is also important.

Some parents may be able to make a direct contribution to the curriculum, by giving talks to groups of children about their work, hobbies or aspects of their culture or religion which may be relevant.

Parents can also be invited to join examination classes as pupils themselves.

Groups or classes can also be set up to provide support for parents. These may relate to general parenting skills, or particular aspects of interest, e.g. helping children with homework, recognising the signs of drug or solvent abuse, issues relating to sex education. A survey could establish the needs of parents in your school community.

Parents' evenings

One of the traditional ways of meeting with parents is at parents' evenings. These are often rather formal occasions, which some parents find intimidating. Their format lends itself to a one-way communication of information from teacher to parent. They are not normally conducive to improving relationships between parents and school.

A number of schools have had considerable success in generating parents' interest in school by setting up more informal workshop or open evenings where the atmosphere has been welcoming. Parents have been able to explore aspects of the curriculum and pupils have displayed work and been available to answer questions about it. Parents have been able to meet teachers in a more informal setting.

An illustration of how a school in Southwark set up an informal parents' evening is given on page 150.

Meetings with parents of individual children

As was indicated in the section on the physical environment of the school, a welcoming entrance hall, with clear signposting of reception areas is important to prevent parents feeling intimidated when making school visits. Providing a special room where meetings with parents can take place is also more welcoming for parents than a meeting held in the office of a member of staff.

Informal parents' evenings

Tables and chairs were set up in a cafe style in the school hall. There were displays of work, videos of children engaged in learning activities, an attendance display, flowers, refreshments and background music. An introductory talk was followed by informal discussion. The meeting lasted from 4 to 6 pm. There was musical entertainment by the lower school choir. Letters and personal invitations were posted to the parents' homes. Staff wore name tags and their photographs were on display. Parents could take part in activities, work with computers, and fill in worksheets. A prize draw was held based on the return of the posted invitation. The evening was very successful.

In some cases, where a visit presents particular difficulties for parents, the school may wish to provide transport. They may also suggest that a leader of a local community group accompanies the parents or provide someone to act as translator.

Another means of encouraging better communication is to arrange for form tutors to have a specified time each week when they are available to meet parents by appointment.

▆▆ Home visits

Home visits are sometimes necessary if parents are unable or unwilling to visit the school. Parents may feel safer and more confident on their home ground. Visiting the home helps the school better understand the child's home situation and relationships within the family. Undertaking a home visit also demonstrates that the school cares about the child.

Attendance officers and social workers regularly visit homes but teachers are often seen as less threatening. Initially, teachers may feel more comfortable making home visits in conjunction with the attendance officer.

If a home visit is to be arranged it is better for it to be undertaken speedily once there are indications of attendance problems. Early positive contact with the home can pave the way for other kinds of visits and may prevent the problem getting worse. It is more difficult to establish good rapport if the problem is long standing. Most home visiting is undertaken during school hours or immediately after school, when a parent is usually at home. The visits are usually short. LEAs have their own guidelines but visits should normally be arranged in advance.

Where this is not possible the visitor should make it plain that they are not expecting to be invited in.

 ## Staff training

Improving relationships with parents requires three main training approaches:

- Changing teachers' attitudes towards the involvement of parents in education;
- The development of communication skills;
- Developing an understanding of the differing life styles of families in the school community.

Involving staff in the planning process to develop stronger links with parents is likely to lead to greater commitment. Staff training time might be set aside to discuss ideas for persuading parents who normally have little contact with school to become more interested in their childrens' education; to consider how staff can more easily be available to meet parents; and to discuss how the school might be made less intimidating for parents.

Education Welfare Officers can provide INSET relating to making home visits and dealing with parents in matters relating to attendance.

Local community leaders can give presentations describing aspects of their culture which may have direct relevance to pupils' attendance and behaviour at school.

12 Home–school links

Summary

Partnerships between parents and school are important for promoting pupil attendance and achievement. To improve links with parents schools can:

- create easy access for parents to meet teachers and form tutors;
- create a welcoming atmosphere for parents;
- invite parents into the school to give presentations;
- make some examination classes available to adults;
- encourage the activities of the Parent Teacher Association;
- value parent governors;
- seek parents' views;
- ensure that communication with parents is frequent, clear, translated into the relevant languages;
- encourage the use of the school for the social activities of both students and parents.

13 School–community links

Families do not exist in isolation. They are part of a wider community within society. If that community is characterised by high unemployment, poverty and alienation from society as a whole, this will inevitably affect children's education.

Unemployment

Unemployment rose rapidly in the 1980s and has remained at a relatively high level since. In areas of very high unemployment there is evidence that many young people simply drop out.[14] They do not feel that they belong in society. Many of the things which most people take for granted: education, qualifications, training, work, career prospects, and a secure income have become irrelevant to them. For some, involvement in crime and anti-social behaviour are their only means of establishing any kind of status or worth. While the education system may offer the opportunity to get qualifications, these are of little use if there is no work available. If whole groups of young people feel that they have been rejected by society in this way, they have nothing to lose by dropping out. Support is then derived from group membership, which becomes closely knit. In these circumstances peer pressure can become very important. If one pupil skips school, they all do. Group membership is so important that behaviour is oriented towards not letting group members down or alienating the individual from the group culture.

Poverty

The number of low paid workers in the UK (based on the Council of Europe's decency threshold of 68 per cent of the mean earnings of all full-time employees) increased by over a quarter to 10 million in 1991. This is almost half of all employees.

There has also been a large increase in the number of one parent families from 850,000 in 1981 to over 4 million in 1990. About one in six families with dependent children are one-parent families. This is due to the large increase in breakdown of relationships and the increase in births outside marriage.

The number of children living in poverty increased to nearly four million or one in three, while the number of children living on the margin of poverty increased to five million, or two in every five children. The risk of poverty is highest in the children of the unemployed, followed by one-parent families and then those in households headed by low paid workers.[23]

Poverty has an adverse effect on health, which in turn also affects educational opportunity. An adverse family and social environment can retard physical, emotional and intellectual growth. There is an increased likelihood of dental decay and a higher incidence of undiagnosed hearing and visual impairment. Schools have been given no additional resources to cope with this.

Children from poor homes often have no breakfast, which can affect concentration in lessons. Living in bed and breakfast accommodation can disrupt children's education and overcrowded accommodation can disturb sleep and create difficulties in doing homework.

Educational implications

There is considerable evidence, collated over many years, that persistent non-attendance at school is related to poverty and general deprivation,[31,4]. Approximately 14 per cent of pupils attend schools located in deprived inner-city areas. 10 per cent of these pupils report serious truancy as against 6 per cent overall. 13 per cent report selective truancy as against 10 per cent overall. Three times as many inner-city secondary schools report serious truancy compared with schools in other areas.

Failure to participate in post-16 education is also linked to poverty. In the majority of the most deprived LEAs, participation rates are well below the national average.

There is also evidence of regional variation in attendance, reflecting differences in tradition, attitudes to education, and the influence of employment and the local economy.[32]

When the country is considered as a whole, educational performance over the past 11 years has improved. However, this improvement has not been even. When the most deprived areas are considered the proportion of school leavers with five or more passes with A–C grades is consistently below the national average. The national average has increased from 24 per cent in 1979/80 to 37.8 per cent in 1990/91. In the most deprived boroughs the relative figures were 14 per cent and 17 per cent. Over the same period, nationally those with no graded results has fallen from 12 per cent to 8 per cent, while there has been little change in the figures for the most deprived boroughs, a drop from 21.5 per cent to 21.1 per cent. In recent years educational attainment between those areas with high and low deprivation scores has widened.[33,34]

Schools, alone, cannot be expected to shoulder the responsibility for remedying problems created by inequalities in society. However, children's attitudes towards school are not directly related to the catchment area of the school[13] and there is evidence[35,36] that even within the same catchment area schools can have different levels of attendance, achievement and delinquency in pupils. So while in some communities, schools cannot be held totally responsible for educational failure, they can, and do have a duty to ameliorate its worst effects.

▓ Improving links with the community

Whatever the circumstances in a school community, its members are generally interested in promoting the well being of the young people within that community. Schools can work in partnership with the community to promote and encourage attendance and achievement at school.

Schools can usefully develop links with religious bodies, ethnic groups, local industry, commerce, ex-pupils' groups, pensioners' groups, and family centres. Links with industry can be particularly important in areas of high unemployment. Direct contact with local employers may facilitate leavers' job prospects and lead to increased motivation at school.

▓ Local residents

Local residents often have concerns regarding pupils' behaviour when they are out of school. Schools can act to reduce fears and promote good relations by encouraging pupils to undertake work in the community. This can take a variety of forms, depending on local circumstances and need. Schools might contribute towards entertainment in old people's homes and local hospitals, or undertake charitable work in the community. Work experience can also be valuable in forging links, particularly where they are related to community work, e.g. in children's nurseries, other local schools, medical centres, libraries, family centres, etc.

The school can also encourage local people to use the school as a centre for their activities. School premises might be made available for cultural events, amateur dramatic society productions, concerts, dancing, etc.

▪▪▪ Links with industry and commerce

Schools can develop and improve links with local industry and commerce through work experience projects and compact schemes. These have already been referred to in relation to the curriculum. Such schemes attempt to promote links which are mutually beneficial.

Local Enterprise Agencies can provide information about local schemes.

▪▪▪ Truancy Watch schemes

Police, local businesses and shopkeepers have been involved in some areas in joint schemes to promote community involvement in improving school attendance. The evidence indicates that such schemes can be effective in the short term.[37] Staff in participating businesses and shops are informed of school dates and times and told how to approach truants. Pupils who need to be out of school during school hours are given a pass which they can show if challenged. Such campaigns receive considerable publicity and are valuable in raising awareness regarding the importance of attendance at school. They may also highlight the vulnerability of truants and the risks they face.

Information from a Truancy Watch scheme

CONTENTS ADVICE SHEET

DOOR STICKERS
To be displayed in a conspicuous place on or near entrance doors facing outwards.

REFERRAL FORMS
It is stressed that these forms should be treated as CONFIDENTIAL DOCUMENTS and are to be kept in a secure place. It is recommended that only security or management have access to these documents.

The forms are to be used to inform the Education Welfare Department when a suspected truant is identified in your premises. Examples of use will be when a truant is detained for a criminal office such as theft or criminal damage. Use of the forms should be in addition to any action involving the Police.

In other cases you will have to be guided by circumstances, but you are reminded that you have no power under law to detain a young person suspected of being a truant in order to establish personal details, and are not encouraged to do so. If, for example, the truant is known to a member of staff, then a form should be forwarded to the Education Welfare Department.

Forms should be forwarded as soon as possible using the self addressed envelopes provided. Copies of the forms should be retained in a SECURE PLACE.

NOTICE TO STAFF
This is a self explanatory guide to the initiative which should be displayed in an area where your staff have access. You are advised to be aware of its contents for your own and necessary training purposes.

SCHOOL INFORMATION SHEETS
These documents contain information relating to local schools such as school holidays, teacher training days and contact names and telephone numbers. These will aid you in identifying truants and should be available to all staff.

PARENTS GUIDES TO TRUANCY
These are provided to inform you of what information has been provided to parents via their children's school.

Staffordshire Police and Education Authority

Dear Proprietor/Manager

TRUANCY INITIATIVE 1993/94

Without doubt education provides our young people with the start in life that they need to develop into responsible citizens. When they fail to take full advantage of the facilities their schools offer they are often labelled as 'truants' and as such not only miss out on their education, but risk becoming involved in crime as participants or victims.

As caring organisations we are all too aware of the effects of crime and feel that we have a responsibility and duty to support and guide our young people.

We have therefore joined together with the theme 'Business Caring for Education' and are to launch a year long initiative commencing in September 1993 with the aim to encourage young people to attend school regularly.

Our methods will include parental advice and talks to the students themselves, utilising both education staff and trained police officers. We also intend to involve the business sector of Hanley in a scheme to discourage truancy in the area. How often do you see children obviously of school years wandering around shops unconcerned and confident that they will not be challenged?

In this pack you are provided with door stickers, information notices, training sheets and referral forms. It is the intention of this initiative that we make young people aware that we care, and on the occasions that they come to notice, make the appropriate authority aware of their presence.

It is not our intention to treat young people failing to attend school as criminals, indeed school children do not commit an offence by failing to attend school. What we wish to do is show that they will be noticed and where appropriate challenged by a member of staff.

As indicated, there are advice and information sheets in your truancy initiative pack. You are urged to study it and follow its advice carefully. Should you require further advice or assistance please do not hesitate to contact the Education Welfare Department, Unity House (Stoke-on-Trent 219611) or the Community Services Department at Hanley Police Station (Stoke-on-Trent 202555).

In conclusion, you are involved in a scheme which if successful will, we are sure, be adopted by other areas both at local and national levels. As a pilot scheme it requires your commitment and understanding. We thank you for your involvement and look forward to working together to improve both the education of our young people and the quality of life in our community.

STOKE-ON-TRENT
CITY CENTRE (HANLEY)
CHAMBER OF TRADE

Supported by: J. H. Brookes Printers, Hanley
and Legs Graphic Design, Leek

Staffordshire
County Council
Pride in your County
Education Welfare Section

NOTICE TO STAFF

Truancy is a problem that affects us all. Not only do truants deprive themselves of valuable education, but they risk becoming involved in crime as participants or victims.

These premises are therefore pledged to support a truancy initiative taking place in this area.

What is a truant? A truant is a young person aged 16 or under. He or she will not be authorised to be absent from school. An authorised absence is, for example, sickness, school holidays, or in rare cases, exclusion from school. It is likely that their parents think they are at school. Many will be truants for the first time . . . we all therefore have a duty to discourage truancy.

DO'S AND DONT'S

DO   Remember truants commit no criminal offence by not attending school.

Remember that you cannot detain a young person for being a truant.

Remember however that you are allowed to question younger customers to establish if they should be at school.

Inform truants that these premises support the truancy initiative, and advise them to return to school.

Be aware of the school holiday timetables available in these premises and refer to them when necessary.

Contact the Police where a child is vulnerable. An example of this would be a child's young age.

DON'T   Get into arguments, be polite and if the suspected truant becomes difficult, call for management, security or, if appropriate, the Police.

Assume that all young people are truants. School holidays differ, and schools close for teacher training days. The young person may have authorised absence from school. However, never be afraid to challenge and ask.

REMEMBER, THESE PREMISES SUPPORT THE EDUCATION AND SAFETY OF YOUNG PEOPLE.

Staffordshire Police and Education Authority

Links with other schools

Liaison between primary and secondary schools is particularly important in relation to attendance. Patterns of absence established in the primary school may continue in the secondary school. Information from the primary school regarding pupils' attendance can be important for instituting preventive work on transfer. The links established between parents and school at primary level also need to be continued on transfer.

Links between primary and secondary schools can be promoted by:

- Joint artistic/musical productions, e.g. concerts, musicals, plays;
- Presentations given at other schools by subject specialists;
- Primary visits to secondary schools for special projects;
- Work experience undertaken in other local schools;
- Liaison on curricula matters;
- Joint planning in relation to school transfer.

Staff training

In promoting links with the wider community it is important that staff receive appropriate training and information. It would be helpful for them to have an understanding of:

- the make up of the community within which the school is located;
- the values of that community;
- knowledge of ethnic, religious, and cultural customs within the community;
- the major types of employment in the area.

Community leaders can be approached to provide information on ethnic, religious and cultural customs. Representatives of local industry and commerce can be invited to the school to describe their work and explore ways that links may be made to the mutual benefit of both parties.

---

13 School–community links

Summary

- Some communities are characterised by unemployment and poverty
- These have been shown to have a negative effect on educational opportunity
- Schools cannot shoulder the entire responsibility for this inequality BUT within the same catchment area schools have different levels of attendance and achievement.
- Schools can and do make a difference
- Schools can assist in improving pupils' attendance by drawing on available resources in the community

They can improve links and form partnerships with:

- Local residents;
- Local industry and commerce;
- Community groups;
- Local primary schools.

Links can be promoted by:

- Making the school available for community events;
- Valuing cultural diversity;
- Forging links with local family and community centres;
- Truancy watch schemes;
- Developing compact schemes.

SECTION V
WAYS OF WORKING
WITH ABSENTEES

14 Working with individuals

Where schools are adopting appropriate procedures to improve attendance, some pupils will be identified whose attendance is particularly erratic or poor.

While schools and LEAs have been successful in returning persistent absentees to school, all concerned agree that it is a difficult task. It is preferable to identify at-risk pupils early, when patterns of non-attendance are first developing, and take preventive measures. The more speedy the intervention the more likelihood there is of success. Schools and LEAs, in a number of projects nationwide, have attempted to identify at-risk pupils and provide support through group work to prevent problems developing (see Chapter 15).

For those individuals exhibiting severe attendance problems, the school will need to initiate specific action. Normally they will be referred to the Education Welfare Service, where individual action plans will be developed. The extent to which the school will be involved in this process will depend on the circumstances of each case. An example depicting typical casework procedures, derived from the City of Coventry, is given below.

Establishing the causes of absence

In establishing the causes of a pupil's absence, it is important to acquire as much relevant information as possible. Interviews with the pupil concerned, their carers and someone who knows the child well in school, can all make a valuable contribution to this process.

School assessment of the individual

An assessment of the school life of the pupil is important for developing a full understanding of their difficulties. It also provides valuable

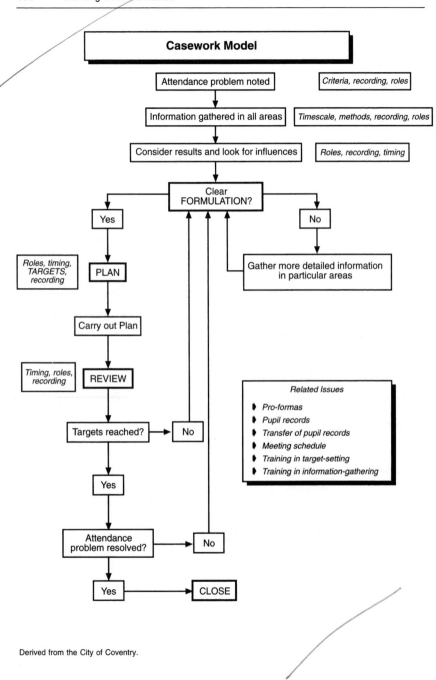

Casework Model

Attendance problem noted → *Criteria, recording, roles*

Information gathered in all areas → *Timescale, methods, recording, roles*

Consider results and look for influences → *Roles, recording, timing*

Clear FORMULATION?

Yes / No

Gather more detailed information in particular areas

Roles, timing, TARGETS, recording

PLAN

Carry out Plan

Timing, roles, recording

REVIEW

Targets reached? → No

Yes

Attendance problem resolved? → No

Yes → CLOSE

Related Issues

▸ *Pro-formas*
▸ *Pupil records*
▸ *Transfer of pupil records*
▸ *Meeting schedule*
▸ *Training in target-setting*
▸ *Training in information-gathering*

Derived from the City of Coventry.

information regarding the nature of the support that they will require on their return to school. An outline of the type of information which has proved useful is given below.

School assessment of the pupil

Details of absence: particular lessons, times, days of week.

School work: national curriculum attainment, basic skill levels, e.g. reading, spelling, writing, mathematics, documented learning difficulties, details of statementing.

Pupil characteristics: strengths, weaknesses, self-esteem and confidence.

Factors believed to contribute to non-attendance: financial, travel, family problems, unemployment, work, health of pupil or others.

Other problems: drugs, drink, solvent abuse, criminal activity.

Work in the classroom: concentration, organisation, motivation, difficulty working in groups or alone, with or without support, curriculum difficulties.

Behaviour in school: relationships with peers and teachers, general behaviour, problems with bullying, negative peer influence.

Agency connections: social work, police, educational psychologists.

Interviews with pupils

Interviews with pupils are essential to fully understand the problems facing the pupil. They should be conducted by someone the pupil sees as trustworthy. It is this relationship which may support the pupil in returning to school. Some suggested questions for the interview, which can act as starting points, are included.

Interviews with parents

The role of parents in cases of persistent absenteeism is often crucial. Interviews conducted with them provide an opportunity for making contact and seeking their views as to possible solutions.

Parents are often reluctant to contact or visit school when their child is not attending regularly. This reluctance may be exacerbated by their own experiences of school. They may also be trying to cope with a range of problems in their personal and family lives which may seem more

Interview questions

Travel

How do you travel to school?

Do you travel alone?

Lessons

Do you have any favourite subjects?

Are there any subjects that you find hard or dislike?

Do you have any favourite teachers? Are there any teachers who you do not get on with?

Do you like working by yourself?

Do you like working in small groups?

Do you like working in large groups or with the whole class?

Which is the best day for being at school and why?

Which is the worst day for being at school and why?

What would you like to get out of school?

How do you feel about starting your option courses?

Pastimes

What are your hobbies and interests?

Are you a member of any clubs or groups?

Friends

Who are your favourite friends outside and inside school?

Are there any children that you don't get on with inside or outside school?

Absenteeism

What happens on a day when you don't go to school?

When did you stop going to school?

Why did you stop going?

Can you remember the first day you skipped a lesson? If yes, why did you do it? What happened?

What would help you to stay in school more?

Family

What does your mum/dad/carer feel about you not attending school?

How are things for you at home?

Does that affect your attendance at school?

The future

If you had a magic wand which could change things, what would it change?

What do you think you'll be doing in 1, 3, and 5 years from now?

Is there anything that you want to ask or anything else that you want to tell me?

important to them than their child's attendance at school. For this reason a visit to their home may be appropriate. Interviews with parents are valuable as they often provide additional information about the absence, suggesting reasons for non-attendance which their child has not mentioned.

Issues that might be raised with parents include:

- Why they think their child is not attending school
- Whether there are any special arrangements which they believe would improve their child's attendance
- Whether the child is being influenced by older siblings
- What action they, or others have taken so far
- What the child does when he or she is not at school

 ## Action

The information collected will indicate the nature of the problem and suggest a plan of action. Whether this involves the home, the school or both, a successful outcome is more likely when all the parties work together. Depending on the severity of the problem the EWO may also be involved.

 ## School action

If the problem is located within the school, e.g. as a result of poor relationships between staff and pupil, bullying or anxiety regarding work, the school can directly implement the necessary plan and monitor its effectiveness.

The particular programme implemented will depend on the circumstances of each case. Where necessary headteachers can make temporary exceptions from the National Curriculum (see DFEE circular 15/89).[38] Some strategies which have been found to be effective, alone or in combination with others, are outlined below. They fall into two main categories relating to social and learning problems.

1. Social problems:

- Social skills training;
- Providing special support during breaktimes;

- Counselling with a trained counsellor;
- Designating an individual member of staff as a mentor.

2. Learning problems:

- Devising a modified timetable;
- Providing additional support in class;
- Arranging a work experience scheme;
- Arranging attendance at a FE college to undertake a vocational course.

The child will require support during this period from someone with whom they have a good relationship. This may be a member of staff, an ancillary or learning support assistant, a school counsellor, a youth worker, or a professional such as an Education Welfare Officer. Whoever undertakes this task will also require appropriate professional support.

In some cases provision for the pupil will be made outside the school, in a group working on attendance issues or at a specified reintegration unit.

Problems outside school

If problems lie outside the school, other agencies will become involved. The nature of the action plan developed will then depend to a great extent on the parents. If they have been unaware of the absence, they may be supportive in getting the child back to school. If they have been aware but unable to do anything about it, they may be glad of school intervention. If they have passively condoned the child's non-attendance then little support can be expected and where absence has actively been encouraged, the school may expect hostility. Often, problems are complicated by disagreement within families.

Schools are identifiers of family difficulties

Schools can often be the first to recognise that a child has problems at home. Family difficulties are not left behind when a child attends school. Problems frequently manifest themselves in behaviour at school. Schools are therefore in an ideal position to recognise children in need of help and may, in consultation with the child, be able to initiate action to provide support from other agencies.

This is particularly true in the case of young carers. They often do not want to reveal their problems for fear of being ridiculed or not believed, especially when the case involves mental illness. They may also be constantly afraid that the adult, or they themselves, will be taken away. Schools routinely note the absence of parents at parents' evenings and children who frequently arrive late or tired. If they are alert to these signs they can identify young carers and offer emotional support, provide access to counselling, and demonstrate flexibility with regard to homework, etc. They can also act to encourage liaison between other agencies to provide support for the child.

Multiple problems

Often problems are multi-faceted, related to poverty, family difficulties, and negative attitudes towards education. In these circumstances pupils may require assistance from several agencies. In some cases, the LEA may feel it necessary to take parents to court.

The legal position

LEAs have a duty to enforce school attendance by serving School Attendance Orders, seeking Education Supervision Orders and taking parents to court, where necessary.

Children themselves are not breaking the law when they stay away from school. The powers of enforcement are only against parents. Under the terms of the 1944 Education Act parents have a duty to ensure that their child receives 'efficient full-time education', according to their 'age, ability and aptitude and any special educational needs he or she may have', while of compulsory school age. This can be 'at school or otherwise'.

Schools are required to inform LEAs of continuous absences of not less than two weeks, except where such absences are covered by a medical certificate. They also have a duty to inform the LEA when pupils do not attend regularly or if they suspect that absence is unauthorised. The DFEE circular of 11/91 further states that 'Schools should develop an effective working relationship with EWOs based on a clearly delineated division of labour'.

School Attendance Orders

School Attendance Orders enable LEAs to serve a notice requiring parents to register their child at a school of their choosing, once it has been established that they are not being properly educated 'other wise'. These orders are only significant in relation to registration at school NOT attendance.

The prosecution of parents

Parents commit an offence if their child fails to attend regularly at the school where they are registered.

The grounds for defence in cases of prosecution are similar to those operating prior to the Education Act, 1993:

- absence 'with leave';
- sickness or other unavoidable cause;
- days of religious observance;
- failure by the LEA to provide transport where required to do so;
- a travelling lifestyle (minimum 200 attendances).

The recent legislation, however, places a greater emphasis on absence with 'leave'. This is granted by someone authorised to do so by the school. If the child is absent with the approval of the school no offence has been committed. This makes decisions by the school regarding the authorisation of absence crucial. If absence is authorised then there are no grounds for prosecution.

A resume of the legal guidelines for granting 'absence with leave' is provided in Section VI. Schools need to be quite clear regarding what constitutes authorised or unauthorised absence.

If there is a court hearing, the head of the school will be required to testify in writing that the attendance record produced is an exact copy of the register. The register is the evidence. Parents may challenge its accuracy.

The evidence regarding the effectiveness of the prosecution of parents, in relation to improving their children's attendance at school, is limited. Many situations seem to deteriorate further after prosecution. Some are unlikely to be resolved by a court case. Prosecution may therefore be of limited use in achieving the main aim, which is to get the child back to school. The Children Act (1989) also requires that attendance problems are viewed within a wider legal framework.

▆▆▆ Children Act (1989)

The Children Act created a new framework for dealing with the welfare of children. Parents' responsibilities are emphasised, with the work of agencies being seen as a service. The Act stresses that parents should be helped to resolve problems on a voluntary basis, and that agencies should work with them in a spirit of partnership. Court action is taken only as a last resort. Children also have a right to be listened to and consulted about major decisions in their lives. The role of agencies is to work together to provide a network of support for children in need.

Those dealing with attendance issues are required to adopt a similar approach. Wherever possible EWOs should resolve issues between the school, the parent and the child without resort to the law. The welfare of the child is in all cases paramount. The model is one of protection and support. LEAs also have a duty to co-operate in providing services to help 'children in need' and their families. This category includes those with attendance problems, excluded children and those at risk of exclusion and those with Special Educational Needs, including emotional and behavioural disorders.

The Children Act set up new courts to deal with law applications regarding children. These Family Proceedings Courts (FPCs) deal with issues relating to children's welfare, e.g. care orders, supervision orders, child protection, and issues relating to divorce and separation. LEAs may now make an application under the Children Act to have a child of compulsory school age placed under its supervision, initially for a period of one year. An Education Supervision Order (ESO) effectively makes the LEA responsible for ensuring that the child is educated, though there is a duty to work closely with both parents and child and take their wishes into account. Applying for an ESO can be undertaken in addition to, or instead of taking proceedings against the parents. But LEAs are required by the law to consider whether an Education Supervision Order is appropriate before prosecuting parents.

▆▆▆ Education Supervision Orders

When an Education Supervision Order is granted, the social worker's responsibility is to befriend the child and his or her family. The intention is not to force the child into school, but rather to encourage and support the child.

To apply for an ESO, records of attendance and written reports describing the strategies already tried are required. These are submitted prior to the court hearing with an action plan outlining what will be done if the order is made, including any proposed changes in educational provision. The court's decision will be based on the best interests of the child. Not attending school is insufficient reason in itself for an order to be made.

The report submitted to the court includes:

1. The child's record of attendance at school;
2. Details of the child's circumstances;
3. An assessment of the causes of poor attendance, including an indication of the attitudes of the pupil and his or her parents;
4. The reasons why the Education Supervision Order is being requested, including an assessment of any harm the child might suffer, should an order not be made;
5. A framework for the intended intervention, including a programme of the proposed work, indicating the role of the child and the parents. This should also indicate why the programme is likely to improve matters and ensure that the child attends school regularly.

The evidence to date indicates that ESOs can be successful in improving a child's attendance at school,[39] particularly when the school, the LEA and other involved agencies work closely together.

Working with other agencies

It is the school's responsibility to monitor pupils' attendance and inform the Education Welfare Service of pupils who do not attend regularly. Where absence is persistent, the school will work with the Education Welfare Officer to assist the child in returning to school. In some cases other agencies will also be involved, e.g. Educational Psychologists.

For effective co-operation with other agencies, school staff must understand their structure, lines of communication, functions and thresholds for accepting referrals. Schools also need to ensure that outside agencies understand how they function.

Links with Education Welfare Officers

Education Welfare Officers or Educational Social Workers, as they are sometimes known are employed by the LEA. Although the Education Welfare Service is not a statutory service, most LEAs have set one up to satisfy legal responsibilities placed upon them by government. The two main functions of EWOs are to investigate the absence of individual children from school and promote good attendance in general. Some Education Welfare Services have adopted a broader role, dealing with issues related to school attendance, e.g. drug use, alcohol abuse, children's employment, child protection issues, bullying. Some, in conjunction with the police and community groups, have set up 'Truancy Watch schemes' (see Chapter 13). In practice there is considerable variability from authority to authority in the range of tasks undertaken.

EWOs can be extremely valuable in helping a school improve attendance, particularly where they are treated as part of the school staff. To assist them in undertaking their duties effectively, the school should provide them with space and appropriate facilities. Where possible they should attend staff meetings and regular consultations should be arranged to discuss individual cases and more general issues relating to attendance. EWOs are a particularly valuable source of feedback regarding the effects of school policies and practices on attendance and disaffection, e.g. school uniform, setting and banding procedures.

With regard to improving general attendance at school, EWOs can:

- talk to pupils in assembly about attendance problems;
- work alongside teachers in PSE lessons and tutor group periods to discuss attendance issues;
- help to set up incentive schemes within the school;
- offer advice on issues related to attendance, e.g. drug abuse, bullying, child employment, etc.;
- participate in short-term absence procedures in the school;
- attend parents' evenings;
- provide in-service training on attendance issues.

In individual cases, EWOs can help in the initial assessment of the situation, gathering information from the pupils, the parents and teachers. They might also observe the child in the classroom setting. They can be invaluable in promoting communication between school and home, setting up meetings, making home visits, explaining school procedures to parents, and discussing their child's school progress. They can also assist teachers in making contact with parents. They also have an important role to play in facilitating links between other outside agencies in relation to particular cases.

In addition to individual casework they may also:

- run drop-in and advice surgeries for pupils with problems;
- run support groups for pupils with attendance problems;
- assist in support units;
- provide information regarding child employment issues;
- carry out random immediate response visits to pupils' homes when absence is unauthorised;
- contribute to work with teenage mothers.

Particularly valuable is work that is undertaken in identifying and working with at-risk pupils. This procedure may begin in the primary school to allow the provision of support groups at the start of secondary school.

The school, in turn, has a responsibility to provide Education Welfare Officers with accurate information regarding pupil attendance. School staff need to be aware of the procedures for referrals to EWOs and follow them consistently. Guidelines, as adopted by Southwark, are presented in the following box.

Educational Psychologists

Educational Psychologists have a role to play in cases where pupils are exhibiting extreme anxiety in relation to school attendance. They can also provide support for individuals with identified difficulties on their transfer from primary to secondary school and assist in developing good communications between their parents and the school.

They also have expertise regarding psychological factors which may affect general attendance levels and can advise schools on motivational issues, reward and punishment systems, classroom interaction, learning difficulties, behavioural policies, social relationships, anxiety in school, bullying, etc. This expertise can be a valuable resource for the provision of in-service training in a range of areas.

Other agencies

In cases of persistent non-attendance a number of other outside agencies may be involved, e.g. health service workers, social workers, youth workers. The children involved in these cases are often among the most vulnerable in society. To minimise the disruption to their education, schools need to maintain close contact with the agencies involved and maximise support for the child.

FOLLOW-UP ACTION IN CASES OF NON-ATTENDANCE

1) In all cases of absence, every effort should be made by the form tutor/teacher to obtain the reason for absence, so that it may be authorised as appropriate. This may involve phone calls home, letters or EO12s being sent to the parents.
The same procedure should be followed in cases where a pupil is persistently late, and in addition the times of arrival should be recorded in the space provided in the register. Pupils should be reminded that being 'too late for a mark' constitutes failure to attend regularly and could lead to prosecution. (Hinchley v Rankin 1961)

2) In obdurate cases, where a child has persistent unauthorised absences, schools should initially invite parents to a meeting to discuss reasons for the absence and possible solutions.

3) Discussions should be taking place concurrently with the school's ESW who can give advice on how the school could deal with the problem. All action taken by the school should be carefully dated and recorded.

4) If, after reasonable efforts by the school to resolve the problem, attendance remains poor, a written referral should be made to the ESWS.

5) Once a decision has been taken by the school and ESW to refer the matter to the ESWS, **it is important that the school informs the parents of this in writing.**

6) The formal referral form E01 should be completed with the fullest information after consultation with the key teaching staff involved with the child, and the ESW or their team manager, and should include details of all action undertaken by the school. An attendance grid indicating the previous 6 weeks' absence should be attached along with a copy of the letter sent to the parents.

7) Once the referral has been accepted by the ESWS it is important that schools continue to work in partnership with the allocated ESW to ensure the child's return to maximum attendance. All members of staff who have contributed to the referral should be kept informed of progress. In cases where an **Education Supervision Order** (under the Children Act 1989) is to be sought in court, the school will normally be involved in the Education Plan for the child and may well have a clear role to fulfil in carrying out that plan.

8) Systems of communication within the school between the Head, teachers and ESW should be efficient in the identification of irregular attendance, and

in the subsequent support offered to children and parents. The better the communication, the more effective the follow-up action will be.

Early identification and effective follow up of non-attendance rely on efficient communication both within the school and between the school and its support services.

Prompt action on non-attendance is an important area of child protection and should also be included in the school Child Protection Policy.

CHILD PROTECTION PROCEDURES

1) **Be aware and alert** – to signs of injury, neglect or distress. The Education Department's circular and procedural guidelines are available for further advice.

2) **Act quickly** – get as much information as possible. Have a quiet word with the child or young person to find our discreetly as much as you can about the circumstances. In the case of suspected sexual abuse, do not question the child – refer to section 2.7 of the procedural guidelines. Make careful notes of what is said to you, including the actual words used.

3) **Share your concerns immediately** – with your Designated Senior Teacher for child protection or Headteacher or Officer-in-Charge who will contact the Duty Social Worker at the appropriate Social Services Department District Office.

YOUR DESIGNATED CHILD PROTECTION SENIOR TEACHER IS:

Derived from Southwark Education Authority

Where a child requires multi-agency support, there can be a tendency for agencies to feel that responsibility lies elsewhere. This can lead to children 'falling through the cracks', a situation, which has been described by Carlen, Gleeson and Wardlaugh[3] as 'circles of blame', each agency or institution blaming the other. Schools can take the lead in minimising such occurrences, by acting as a centre, co-ordinating liaison between the agencies, to ensure that the best interests of the child are served.

Regular meetings between the representatives of the differing agencies involved in difficult cases, not only provide opportunities for an exchange of ideas in relation to that case but also discussion on broader issues. Such inter-agency meetings can enable at risk children to be identified more easily, facilitating preventive intervention and leading to useful exchanges of ideas.

How can schools actively improve liaison? Within the school named members of staff can be given particular responsibility for liaison with particular groups of professionals. In individual cases, a named member of staff can be given responsibility for the issues arising in relation to one child. Schools can also convene regular meetings of involved professionals and promote open forums where representatives of the agencies can air and discuss common problems and generate ideas to solve them.

Returning to school after a period of absence

The longer children are out of school, the harder it becomes for them to return. Going back to school after a long period away is often traumatic. The pupil will almost inevitably face problems. But schools can adopt strategies which will help the child to successfully overcome these difficulties and return to a normal pattern of school attendance.

When a child returns to school after a long period of absence it is crucial that school staff are involved in the planning process. Persistent absentees can be regarded as pupils with Special Educational Needs, which means that a special programme can be tailored to meet their individual needs and requirements. This may involve phased, part-time re-entry and/or the provision of additional staff support. Staff throughout the school also need to be made aware of the kinds of difficulties that pupils experience on their return.

School work

Returners usually experience problems in catching up with the work that they have missed. Schools can support them in this by:

- providing a place to carry out private study;
- negotiating a reduced timetable;
- selecting core areas of the curriculum for concentrated work;
- encouraging parental support with homework;
- providing a member of staff to give individual help.

School routine

Readjusting to school routine can be difficult. The size of the building and the number of pupils can be threatening and the organisation and routine of school may prove demanding. The school day can seem very long and relating to the differing teaching styles and personalities of the teachers can be difficult. Movement between classes may be a constant source of temptation to leave school.

In addition to the problems of adjustment to school, the routine of getting up and leaving the house in the morning will have been lost.

A number of strategies can be adopted by schools to assist pupils. They can:

- arrange for the pupil to visit the school prior to their return to overcome their initial fears, preferably when the building is empty;
- provide a written reminder of the school timetable, teachers' names and rules;
- allow part-time attendance, initially.

Social readjustment

Often on a return to school after a long absence pupils experience feelings of isolation and an inability to relate to their peer group and/or teachers. Friendship groups and other aspects of the the social make up of their class may have changed. They may also have to face constant enquiries and comments about where they have been from staff and pupils. These can be extremely difficult to cope with. It is helpful if staff and pupils make positive responses to their return, conveying the message 'We are glad that you are here'.

Staff need to be made aware of the pupil's imminent return and of any special arrangements which may have been made to facilitate a smooth readjustment. They must also be made aware that sensitivity is required in dealing with the child, and that they should avoid making sarcastic comments and jokes at the pupil's expense.

Discussion in the child's tutor group prior to their return is useful to prepare the class. Some schools also present welcome back cards to returning pupils.

The child also needs to be prepared for possible problems. Role play of difficult situations prior to returning to school can be particularly beneficial, as can more general training in social skills.

Providing general support

The provision of a mentor who is able to offer regular daily contact has proved to be an extremely effective way of supporting pupils returning to school after a long absence. The pupil reports to the mentor twice a day during school and makes additional contact if there are any difficulties. The mentor should be somebody to whom the pupil can easily relate.

In some cases it has been possible to provide counselling provision to assist the child and his or her family through this period.

Reintegration units have been set up in some schools enabling pupils to undertake a phased re-entry to school. Such units offer small group work and operate in less formal circumstances, often with a reduced timetable and reduced overall attendance.

Education Welfare Assistants, young people who have themselves experienced problems with school attendance, can also be helpful

 Monitoring progress

During a return to school the child's progress needs to be monitored. Time should be made available for meetings of the head of year, form tutor, EWOs, parents and the pupil. If the child's difficulties are overwhelming and the return is not going smoothly schools may wish to explore other alternatives.

Staff training

Procedures for dealing with persistent absentees are a whole-school concern. Staff at all levels should be familiar with the legal position, the way that outside agencies work and the problems that pupils experience on their return to school.

Schools can approach representatives of outside agencies to provide training. This has the additional benefit of strengthening links between school staff and the agencies. Such approaches may be beneficial with Education Welfare Officers, Educational Psychologists, social workers, youth workers, representatives of behaviour support services and special units in the area. Staff might also find it useful to have information about family support centres, family therapy and child guidance centres, home tuition services and traveller children support groups.

In addition to outlining their own procedures and practices, representatives from these groups might present in-service training days on:

- education supervision orders;
- the Children Act (1989);
- child employment;
- school phobia and school refusal;
- child carers;
- child protection issues;
- drug abuse;
- bullying;
- traveller children;
- truancy watch schemes;
- exclusion from school.

As legislation and practices change over time schools can consolidate links with outside agencies by requesting their assistance in updating knowledge, procedures and practices.

---

14 Working with individuals

Summary

Prevention is better than cure

If problems have arisen, intervention is more likely to be effective if:

- problems are identified quickly;
- action is based on an understanding of the circumstances;
- an action plan is implemented as soon as possible before matters deteriorate;
- other agencies are involved as necessary;
- other involved agencies and the school work closely together;
- progress is reviewed regularly and plans revised if necessary;
- appropriate procedures are implemented to support children on their return to school;
- opportunities are provided for staff training.

15 Working with groups

Throughout this book, the importance of preventive measures has been stressed. Where possible children who are beginning to exhibit patterns of erratic attendance should be identified and measures implemented to deal with the problem before it becomes entrenched. Group work is particularly valuable in this respect. Working with groups is less time consuming than working with individual pupils and has the added advantage of utilising peer pressure. A number of schools and authorities have set up groups which target poor attenders.

The type of group work or scheme adopted depends on the nature of the problem. Group work may be undertaken within one school, or members may be drawn from several schools. In some cases the meetings of the group may be central to the intervention, in others peripheral, e.g. in work placement schemes. When group activities are central, a number of factors relating to group work need to be considered.

General guidelines

Groups need to have a specific purpose. Without a particular aim they lack direction. Motivation can be difficult to sustain in both pupils and staff. While the overall aim might be quite general, for instance, to improve attendance or literacy skills, more specific objectives might also be identified, e.g. to achieve 80 per cent attendance, to take an external literacy examination. Concrete goals such as these are measurable and can provide pupils with a great sense of achievement when they are attained. For pupils experiencing problems at school, success may normally be rather limited, making it all the more important in the group situation.

Working in groups utilises peer support, takes advantage of positive peer group pressure and encourages the development of social skills and techniques of social negotiation. Groups can provide a safe environment for learning life and coping skills and practising problem solving techniques. They also enable young people to pool resources.

For group work to be successful pupils must be willing to participate and be prepared to derive benefit from the group. Parental support of group membership is also very important. However if the pupil is keen to participate and parental support is not forthcoming, the opportunity for the pupil to participate should not be denied.

Most successful groups have around 10 pupils. Groups are usually made up of pupils of a similar age. Often it is better if they are single sex. This provides more opportunities for open discussion of issues relevant to each gender, without the inhibiting presence of a member of the opposite sex.

To be effective the group must meet at least once a week, at a regular time to encourage good attendance. Timing will depend on the nature of the group. If it is within a single school it may meet after school, in tutor group time or PSE lessons. Groups need to meet for about 90 minutes to be effective. This tends to preclude them being held at lunchtime.

Where pupils are already persistent absentees it may be necessary to lay on transport to ensure their attendance. If members miss a session it is essential that the absence is followed up immediately.

Staffing

Groups can be staffed by any professional with the relevant expertise. If the group is particularly concerned with attendance issues this may be an Education Welfare Officer, a teacher, a youth worker, a home–school link worker, an Educational Psychologist, a social worker or a member of another professional agency. At least one member of staff should have experience of group work. If the group is to be of mixed gender, there should be representatives of each gender in the make up of staff.

Staff must be given sufficient time to plan meetings, and monitor and review progress. They must agree on issues relating to style of leadership and the ways that they will deal with conflict, confrontation and difficult situations in advance. In addition to the group leader and group workers, an outside professional will normally act as consultant, working in an advisory capacity. They will normally not attend the group or organise its day-to-day running.

▄▄▄ Activities

The programme of activity undertaken in the group will vary depending on the purpose of the group. Whatever the aim of the group, the first session should provide opportunities for the participants to get to know each other. This is essential if they are to function as a group rather than a set of individuals.

A variety of techniques can be used in groups to facilitate an appropriately relaxed atmosphere. It is useful if refreshments can be provided or there are facilities for making them. Informal teaching techniques using role play, group discussion, videos, tapes, work with cartoons can be particularly useful but for some tasks formal techniques may be appropriate.

The pupils in the group will have generally experienced little success in school. Group activities should therefore endeavour to build confidence and self-esteem, increase self-awareness and provide opportunities to succeed.

In addition to group activity, sessions should be arranged with individuals to enable them to discuss issues which they may not feel comfortable raising with the whole group.

Some schools have also adopted a system of 'befriending' where senior pupils tutor year 7 pupils, believed to be at risk of non-attendance from their records in primary school.

▄▄▄ Issues for discussion

Initial session should first create an appropriate atmosphere where group members feel that they can communicate freely. Later sessions focusing on attendance can deal with:

- the importance of attending school for acquiring qualifications and getting a job;
- the negative consequences, for themselves and their parents, of non-attendance;
- the legal position regarding non-attendance at school;
- their reasons for non-attendance at school;
- the practical aspects of domestic routine which affect attendance, e.g. getting up in time;
- problems they may be experiencing at school;
- leisure activities;
- relationships with peers and staff.

▇ Other groups

Other groups related to improving attendance include:

▇ Groups to improve relationships

Difficulties with relationships often underlie non-attendance at school. Pupils can experience problems in relationships with teachers, authority figures in general, parents or their peers. Such difficulties can also be important in relation to exclusion from school. Establishing groups which assist pupils with social skills can therefore be extremely valuable. Groups can work together to generate ideas for handling potentially difficult situations in school and devise individual coping strategies. Brainstorming, discussion, and role play have all been successfully used for this purpose. It is particularly helpful for pupils to take on the role of the teacher. This can lead to an understanding of the teacher's predicament.

▇ Basic skills groups

Pupils who skip school often do so because they are experiencing difficulties with the curriculum, because of a lack of basic skills. Where schools have set up groups to improve basic literacy, raising reading ages and improving writing and mathematics skills, pupils have become more confident and attendance has improved. Work in small groups with additional individual support has been particularly successful. Reward systems for positive behaviour and progress have helped to improve concentration. Particularly successful has been providing an outing for the whole group when sufficient points have been accumulated. This has the effect of increasing group pressure on individuals to pull their weight.

Alternative basic skills examinations have also proved extremely valuable as motivators for those in year 11 with no GCSE examinations to take.

▇ Homework groups

The domestic circumstances of some pupils are such that they have nowhere at home suitable for doing homework. Non completion of homework can be a factor in deterring pupils from attending school. Setting up a homework club, where a member of staff is on hand to help with problems can assist in improving attendance. Such clubs are particularly successful when computer facilities are available so that work can be undertaken using word processing packages, etc.

Pre-vocational groups

Where pupils are experiencing difficulties with the national curriculum, some schools have successfully developed pre-vocational courses, e.g. travel and tourism, environmental studies. These short courses have been timetabled for about three hours a week and have been useful for increasing motivation, which has extended into other curriculum subjects.

Other schools have explored setting up 12 week courses, where pupils undertake practical work activity for one day a week, for instance, painting and decorating for a charitable institution. Such opportunities, give disaffected pupils the opportunity to acquire useful skills, improve motivation, increase self-esteem and improve attendance at school.

Work schemes

In conjunction with local industry and commerce, schemes have been developed, e.g. STEP (School Time Enterprise Programme), which aim to enhance the range of educational opportunities available to young people in their last years of compulsory schooling. These schemes are aimed at those young people who are already disaffected, poor attenders and at risk of exclusion. The schemes aim to increase motivation and the employment prospects of the participants. School attendance is combined with part-time vocational experience.

Placements are underpinned by agreement between pupils, school, employer and parents. The agreement requires that the work placement depends on regular school attendance. In some cases it may also depend on the cessation of criminal activity. Details of the scheme and the achievements of the young person while undertaking it are included in the pupils record of achievement.

Such schemes have shown considerable success. The pupils taking part demonstrate increased maturity and in the majority of cases improved attendance. Placements are arranged with local employers, after discussion with the pupil and his or her parents, as to what might be appropriate. They are for one day a week for a year. A variety of different placements have been made, e.g. plasterer, dental laboratory assistant, public sector worker, hairdresser, shop assistant, nursery assistant, garage mechanic.

While some students have found the remaining four days a week at school difficult, others have realised that they need qualifications to improve their job prospects and have become better motivated. Where necessary individual learning programmes have been developed to provide pupils with the particular skills that they feel will be valuable.

For such schemes to be successful, schools need to provide support for the pupils. The group involved in the project need to meet together for at least an hour each week to discuss experiences and any difficulties they may be having. Staff organising the project also need time to undertake their duties properly.

Outward bound groups

In some places where poor attenders also have problems in the community, the police, in conjunction with other agencies, have organised weekend outward bound projects. Before participating, pupils must achieve particular targets relating to attendance, punctuality, and schoolwork, which are set out in a contract. A training course must also be completed before the trip.

Reintegration groups or units

There are differing views about the value and appropriateness of re-integration units and groups. Each school must establish the balance which is appropriate for its circumstances at the time, between support in the classroom, phased reintegration and separate provision.

Returning to school after a period of absence can be difficult for pupils. If schools have reintegration groups or units they are formalising this process. Reintegration may take a considerable time. Sometimes it is impossible. Some pupils feel happier working in a unit where they are in a small group and can receive individual help in a secure environment.

Even where schools do not have reintegration units, a number have found it useful to provide a support room, which offers pupils space, opportunities for time-out, and support if they require it.

Family groups

The families of persistent absentees often appreciate being able to join a family support group. Parents often feel that they face insurmountable problems in dealing with difficult young people and welcome opportunities to discuss their situation in a supportive environment. If possible, family sessions should be linked to group work being undertaken by pupils.

Project for disaffected pupils in Corby

The project was set up for disaffected non-attenders to provide a bridge back to school. Those involved came from families with multiple social problems, most receiving support from several agencies. Some were known offenders. Most were insecure, unhappy and lacked confidence in themselves and others.

Many of the students were weak academically, so the curriculum focused on basic skills. It was clearly structured with regular weekly tests providing measurable evidence of progress. The teaching was carried out in small groups, where pupils received individual attention. Pupils were able to take successfully Associated Examining Board Achievement Tests in Numeracy and Literacy and Basic Tests in English, Arithmetic and Life Skills. This gave them a great sense of achievement. In general, however, educational qualifications proved meaningless compared with the street credibility associated with drugs and money.

The development of social skills and the building of relationships with each other and adults was seen as a priority for most pupils, in particular learning the skills of negotiation and compromise. The group also focused on difficulties at school and dealing with authority figures. Behaviour improvement was seen as crucial. Self awareness, assessment and appraisal exercises were used regularly. A behaviourist approach was adopted, rewards being given for positive behaviour, attendance, punctuality, effort in work, and consideration for others. Letters to parents, attendance certificates and the earning of privileges were used to reinforce good behaviour.

Pupils, after making progress, did not want to leave the group and return to mainstream school. Even when the school made enormous efforts to reintegrate them and provide them with support, it remained difficult for them to succeed in that environment, as it was impossible to provide sufficient individual attention.

Overall, the project was successful in improving attendance, and social behaviour, an all-girls group being particularly effective. The project provided a useful educational experience where previously there had been none and pupils left the education system on a positive note with their self-esteem raised.

Stephenson Way Education Project, Corby, Northamptonshire

Family groups can assist parents in gaining confidence in their parenting skills and themselves. They enable parents to share ideas about how to communicate effectively with their children, improve relationships and gain understanding of their offspring. They can also provide opportunities for role play and developing skills for dealing with difficult behaviour. Groups can be particularly valuable for parents of children who are the subject of an Education Supervision Order.

If such groups are set up, providing creche facilities may encourage parents to attend. It may be possible for these facilities to be shared with those for pregnant teenage mothers.

Teenage pregnancy

Attendance at school is often a problem for teenage mothers. In some cases it may have been problematic before they became pregnant, but the responsibilities of motherhood often exacerbate this. Providing creche facilities can help. These can also be used for parents' support groups.

Staff training

Working with groups of disaffected pupils requires considerable skill. Staff wishing to undertake such work will need training related specifically to group work. They may also wish to undertake counselling training. At a more general level, for understanding how such groups operate, representatives of local agencies or teachers working in the field may be willing to provide INSET sessions.

15 Working with groups
Summary

Group work can be preventive or remedial.

Groups can be set up within a single school or across schools.

Groups can be set up for:

■ at-risk pupils;

■ persistent absentees;

■ parents.

To be effective groups should be:

■ small;

■ have a specified interest or focus;

■ be led by someone with experience;

■ provide support.

Groups can focus on:

■ attendance issues;

■ social skills;

■ basic skills;

■ reintegration.

Working effectively with groups requires considerable expertise and training.

SECTION VI
USEFUL
INFORMATION

References

1. Ellis, A.C.O. (1973) 'Influences on school attendance in Victorian England', *British Journal of Educational Studies*, 21, 131–326.
2. Murgatroyd, S. (1987) 'Combating truancy: A counselling approach', in K. Reid (Ed.), *Combating school absenteeism*, Hodder and Stoughton, London.
3. Carlen, P., Gleeson, D. & Wardlaugh, J. (1992) *Truancy: The politics of compulsory schooling*, Open University, Buckingham.
4. University of North London Truancy Unit, Truancy Research Project (1994) *Truancy in English Secondary Schools: A Report for the DFE by the Truancy Research Project, 1991–1992*, University of London Truancy Unit, HMSO, London.
5. Barber, M. (1994) *Young people and their attitudes to school: An interim report of a research project*, Centre for successful schools: Keele University.
6. Gray, J. & Jesson, D. (1990) *Truancy in Secondary Schools amongst fifth year pupils*, QQSE Research Group, Sheffield University.
7. Bealing, V. (1990) 'Inside information: Pupil perceptions of absenteeism in the secondary school', *Maladjustment and Therapeutic Education*, 8(1), 19–34.
8. Kennedy, W.A. (1965) 'School phobia: rapid treatment of 50 cases', *Journal of Abnormal Psychology*, 70, 285–298.
9. Whitney, I. & Smith, P. (1993) 'A survey of the nature and extent of bullying in junior/middle and secondary schools', *Educational Research*, 35, 3–25.
10. Cohen, R., Hughes, M., Ashworth, L. & Blair, M. (1994) *School's out: The family perspective on school exclusion*, Family Service Units/Barnardos, London.
11. Stirling, M. (1993) 'A black mark against him: Why are African-Caribbean boys over-represented in the excluded pupil population?', *Multicultural Education Review*, 15, 3-6.

12. Trenchard, C. & Warren, H. (1987) 'Talking about school: The experiences of young lesbians and gay men', in G. Weinder & M. Arnot (Eds), *Gender under scrutiny: New inquiries in education*, Open University/Hutchinson, London.

13. Keys, W. & Fernandes, C. (1993) *What do students think about school? Research into the factors associated with positive and negative attitudes towards school and education*, NFER, Slough.

14. Wilkinson, G. (1994) *Young people: A chance to be heard – A study of school, training and 'dropping out' in Sunderland, with particular reference to the Ford and Pennywell area*, A research project funded by the Employment Service and the Ford and Pennywell Advice Centre.

15. Morrow, V. (1992) *A sociological study of the economic role of children, with particular reference to Birmingham and Cambridgeshire*, Unpublished PhD thesis, Cambridge University.

16. McKechnie, J., Lindsay, S. & Hobbs S. (1993) *Child employment in Cumbria: A report to Cumbria County Council*, Paisley, University of Paisley.

17. Clwyd, A. (1994) *Children at risk: an analysis of illegal employment of children in Great Britain*, Labour Party Report, Ann Clwyd, London.

18. Harris, S. & Ruddick, J. (1993) 'Establishing the seriousness of learning in the early years of secondary school', *British Journal of Educational Psychology*, 63, 322–336.

19. Office for Standards in Education (1993) *Achieving good behaviour in schools: A report from the Office of Her Majesty's Chief Inspector of Schools*, HMSO, London.

20. Ames, C. (1992) 'Achievement goals and the classroom motivational climate', in D. Schunk & J. Meece (Eds.), *Student perception in the classroom*, Lawrence Erlbaum, Hillsdale, NJ; Hove.

21. Epstein, J. (1989) 'Family structures and student motivation: A developmental perspective', in C. Ames & R. Ames (Eds), *Research on motivation in education*, Vol. 3, Academic Press, New York.

22. Dowswell, T. & Hewison, J. (1995) 'Schools, maternal employment and child health care', *British Educational Research Journal*, 21(1), 15–29.

23. Kumar, V. (1993) *Poverty and inequality in the UK: the effects on children*, National Childrens Bureau, London.

24. O'Neill, A. (1988) *Young carers: The Thameside research*, Thameside Metropolitan Borough Council.

25. Page, R. (1988) *Report on the initial survey investigating the number of young carers in Sandwell secondary schools*, Sandwell Metropolitan Borough Council.

26. Baarda, D.B. (1988) *Schoolprestaties van kinderen van werkloze vaders*

(*School performances of children of unemployed fathers*) with a summary in English, Rijks University of Utrecht, Unpublished PhD thesis.

27. Oakley, C.A. (1936) 'Some psychological problems of a depressed area', *Human Factor*, 10, 393–404.

28. DES (1989) *Attendance at school: A report by HM Inspectorate, Education Observed no. 13*, Department of Education and Science, London.

29. Fletcher Campbell, F.J. & Hall, C. (1991) *Changing schools? changing people? A study of the education of children in care*, NFER-Nelson, Slough.

30. Department for Education, Circular 13/94. *The Education of Children being looked after by Local Authorities*, DFEE, London.

31. Grimshaw, R.H. & Pratt, J.D. (1986) 'Counting the absent scholars: some implications for managerial practice arising from a survey of absenteeism in a city's secondary schools, *School organization*, 6(1), 155–173.

32. Department of Education and Science (1989) *Education Observed 13: Attendance at School*, DES, A report by HMI, London.

33. DES Statistics of Education: School Leavers CSE and GCSE, annual publications until 1988 in Kumar, V., (1993) *Poverty and inequality in the UK: the effects on children*, National Childrens Bureau, London.

34. Department for Education (1991b) *School Examination Survey 1989/90 Statistical Bulletin*, 22/91, December.

35. Reynolds, D., Jones, D., St Leger, S. & Murgatroyd, S. (1980) 'School factors and truancy, in L. Hersov & I. Berg (Eds), *Out of school*, John Wiley, Chichester.

36. Rutter, M., Maughan, B., Mortimore, P. & Ouston, J. (1979) *Fifteen Thousand Hours, Secondary schools and their effects on children*, Open Books, London.

37. West, D.J. (1982) *Delinquency; its roots, careers, and prospects*, Heinemann, London

38. Department of Education and Science, Circular 15/89, *Education Reform Act 1988: Temporary exceptions from the national curriculum* DES, London.

39. Whitney, B. (1994) *The truth about truancy*, Kogan Page, London.

Summary of DFEE guidelines on attendance

Categorising school absence as authorised or unauthorised

This section gives a brief resume of the guidelines regarding school attendance presented in *School Attendance: Policy and practice on categorisation of absence* published by the DFEE (1994). As the booklet makes clear, the guidelines do not constitute an authoritative interpretation of the law. That is exclusively a matter for the courts.

Parents' responsibilities

Parents and guardians are required to ensure that children of compulsory school age receive efficient full-time education. This means that they are responsible for ensuring that children attend and stay at school unless alternative arrangements for their education are made. They are also responsible for informing schools of any absence as soon as possible, ideally on the first day of absence. They should state the nature of the illness and when the child is expected to return to school.

How this contact is made should be decided by the school. Telephone calls, letters or personal contact are acceptable. The school should also state their attendance policy at parents' meetings, in the prospectus and at other opportunities, e.g. when letters are sent home.

Schools should ensure that parents are:

- reminded of their statutory duties;
- aware of the school's requirements as regards notification of absence.

Registration

Schools, other than independent schools for boarders, must keep an attendance register on which at the *beginning* of each morning and after-noon session, pupils are marked present or absent. The absence must be registered as authorised or unauthorised.

Registers must be kept accurately as they may be used in evidence in cases where parents are being prosecuted for school attendance offences.

Where post-registration truancy is a problem, head teachers may wish to institute the taking of class registers at the beginning of each lesson.

The format of registers is left to individual schools but consistency of registration practice is vital. All teachers within the school must oper-ate to the same rules.

Written registers must be kept in ink and corrections made in such a way that the original and the correction are both clearly visible. Corrections must also be distinguishable in computer systems and a print-out must be made at least once a month. The print-outs must be bound into annual volumes as soon as practicable after the end of the school year and retained for three years.

The education welfare system

LEAs are charged in law with enforcing school attendance. The LEA can apply to the courts for an Education Supervision Order and, where necessary, they can prosecute the parents.

Schools should develop an effective working relationship with EWOs based on a clearly delineated division of labour.

LEAs should be informed of attendance problems. *All* schools must report to their LEA on continuous absences of not less than two weeks and on those pupils who fail to attend regularly, except where such absences are covered by a medical certificate.

Categorising absence

Parents can be prosecuted under the Education Act of 1993 for failing to ensure their child's attendance at school with the following exceptions:

- the pupil was absent with permission from an authorised person within school;
- the pupil was ill or prevented from attending by an unavoidable cause;

- the absence occurred on a day exclusively set aside for religious observance by the religious group to which the family belongs;
- the school is not within walking distance of the home and no suitable arrangements have been made for transport to school, boarding accommodation or enabling the child to be registered at a school nearer his home.

There are also some exceptions for the children of travellers.

Notes from parents

The school should specify the means of notifying absence. Only the *school* can approve absence not parents. The school does not have to accept the parents' offered explanation as a valid reason for absence. If there are doubts about the explanation the absence must be treated as unauthorised.

Illness, medical and dental appointments

Such absences are considered authorised providing that the school is satisfied that the illness, appointments, etc. are genuine.

Lateness

Schools should discourage lateness. Schools may keep their registers open for a reasonable time (recommended maximum 30 minutes). Where pupils miss registration and fail to provide an adequate explanation they should be marked as unauthorised absent for that session. If a person does arrive late and misses registration this must be noted for the purposes of emergency evacuation.

Minding the house/looking after brothers and sisters

This is an area where schools have discretion. The Secretary of State would not expect schools to grant leave except in exceptional circumstances. Most cases will be *unauthorised absence*.

Shopping during school hours

It is highly unlikely that such absence can ever be justified.

Special occasions

It is for the school to determine whether an absence in this category should be authorised or not. It will clearly depend on the circumstances.

Family bereavements

Schools should respond sensitively to requests for leave of absence to attend funerals or associated events. They have discretion to authorise such absences. Where a pupil is absent for more than the agreed period early contact should be made with the family.

Family holidays and extended trips overseas

There is discretionary power for leave to be granted for the purpose of an annual family holiday or a holiday during term time. Only in exceptional circumstances may the amount of leave granted exceed two weeks. No parent can demand leave of absence for the purposes of a holiday. Periods of more than two weeks are considered as exceptional. Where holidays of more than two weeks are planned to visit overseas relatives the school may find it helpful to discuss with the parents the best timing for the trip from an educational point of view.

Days of religious observance

An offence is not committed where the absence results from participation in a day set aside exclusively for religious observance by the religious body to which the parents belong.

Traveller children

Travellers are protected from prosecution if they can show that the nature of their trade requires travel from place to place and that the child has attended school as regularly as possible. Where the child has attained the age of 6 years, he/she should have made at least 200 attendances during the previous 12 months.

Interviews

Where a child attends a job interview or application for a place at an institution of further or higher education the school has discretion to authorise the absence. Schools should expect and ask for advance notification.

Work experience and public performances

Leave of absence may be granted for work experience or to participate in approved public performance. If the student is then absent from the work experience or performance this will constitute unauthorised absence.

Off-site activities

These fall into two categories, (1) school directed, e.g. educational visits and (2) individual activities, e.g. music examinations, etc. School activities will normally be registered as absent. Where a small group is involved and not at the place of normal registration such absences will be classed as authorised.

Where the activity is of a more individual nature the school can authorise absence at its discretion. If a registered pupil requires special off-site tuition leave of absence may be granted and the absence treated as authorised.

Excluded pupils

Where a pupil has been temporarily excluded he or she should remain on the school roll. This should be treated as authorised absence. If a pupil has been excluded permanently his absence should be treated as authorised until after review. Once the exclusion is confirmed he or she should be struck off the school roll.

Pupils at pupil referral units

Off-site units are required to keep attendance records. Provision is made for dual registration to facilitate return to main stream. The pupil must be classified as authorised absent when he or she is not attending. Arrangements of this kind need to be formalised in writing.

Study leave

Only year 11 pupils should be granted study leave. It should be granted sparingly, normally with a maximum of two weeks.

School leaving date

Pupils are required to remain at school until the relevant leaving date. Any absence not agreed in advance must be treated as unauthorised.

KEY POINTS

- Registered pupils of compulsory school age are required by law to be in school;
- The aim of schools should be to expect regular attendance, even when schools recognise the problems of individual families and children;
- Lateness should be discouraged;
- Where a pupil is absent without prior permission an explanation is required. If one is not forthcoming the absence must be treated as unauthorised;
- Schools are not obliged to accept parental notes where there is reasonable doubt as to the validity of the explanation;
- Explanations such as minding the house, looking after children, shopping, etc. will not normally be accepted as reasons for absence;
- Parents should not expect, as of right, that schools will agree to family holidays in term time. Each application must be considered on its merits;
- Even where absence is authorised schools should be alert to emerging patterns of absence which may seriously disrupt continuity of learning;
- In promoting regular attendance schools should work closely with Educational Welfare Officers.

Further reading and sources of information

Sources of information and help

General

Local sources include LEAs, universities, commercial providers of in-service training, and staff development co-ordinators. Information about national courses may be obtained from professional journals, papers and magazines.

In addition the following may be useful as providers of in-service training and general advice on truancy-related issues.

University of North London Truancy Unit, School of Teaching Studies, University of North London, Marlborough Building, 383 Holloway Rd, London N7 0RN, 0171 753 5753.

Leeds Attendance Project (co-ordinator Ros Jones), Bentley Primary School, Bentley Lane, Leeds, LS6 4AJ, 01532 307561.

This group can provide information on attendance issues and materials for in-service training.

National Council for Educational Technology, Milburn Hill Road, Science Park, Coventry, CV4 7JJ, 01203 416994.

NCET can provide advice on computerised registration packages.

Association of Chief Education Social Workers, Bank House, 76 Nutgrove Rd, Nutgrove, St Helens, 0151 430 0112.

Persistent absentees

Cities in Schools, 60–1 Trafalgar Square, London, WC2N 5DS, 0171 839 2899.

Cities in Schools offer a range of services aimed at preventing or remedying pupils' disaffection and truancy. Schemes include initiatives in primary and secondary schools, bridge courses for young people who have completely dropped out of school or been excluded, and summer schools providing educational and vocational courses in deprived areas during school holidays.

Local Education and Business Partnerships or Local Training and Enterprise Councils (TEC) will have information on COMPACT, COMPACT PLUS and STEP schemes.

◼ School Effectiveness and Improvement Centres

These provide consultancy services and in-service training in relation to school improvement.

Centre for Successful Schools, Department of Education, Keele University, Keele, Staffordshire, ST5 5BG, 01772 621111.

Improving the Quality of Education for All Project, Cambridge Institute of Education, Shaftsbury Rd, Cambridge, CB2 2BX, 01223 69631.

International School Effectiveness and Improvement Centre, Institute of Education, University of London, Bedford Way, London WC1H 0AL, 0171 612 6347.

Centre for School Improvement, School of Education, University of Bath, BA2 7AY, 01225 826334.

Centre for Research and Consultancy, Faculty of Education, University of Strathclyde, Jordanhill Campus, 76 Southbrae Drive, Glasgow, G13 1PP, 0141 950 3168/3369.

◼ Truancy

Booklets giving information about school attendance

Children out of school: a guide for parents and schools on non-attendance at school, Advisory Centre for Education, London.

Education Observed 13: attendance at school, HM Inspectorate Publication.

School Attendance: Policy and practice on categorisation of absence; Department for Education, London.

Access, achievement and attendance in secondary schools (1995), Office for Standards in Education, London.

The challenge for education welfare, (1995) Office for Standards in Education, London.

Haigh, G. (1993) *Using technology to combat truancy*, City Technology Colleges Trust Limited, London.

MacBeath, J. (1995) *The truancy file*, Quality in Education, Centre for Research and Consultancy, University of Strathclyde, A resource pack for schools.

Available books raising issues related to truancy

Carlen, P., Gleeson, D & Wardlaugh, J. (1992) *Truancy: The politics of compulsory schools,* Open University Press, Buckingham.
Hallam, S. & Roaf, C. (1995) *Here today, here tomorrow: Helping schools to promote attendance,* Calouste Gulbenkian Foundation, London.
O'Keefe, D.J. (1993) *Truancy in English Secondary Schools,* HMSO, London.
O'Keefe, D.J. & Stoll, P. (Eds) (1995) *Issues in school attendance and truancy,* Pearsons Professional, Southport.
Whitney, B. (1994) *The truth about truancy,* Kogan Page, London.
LeRitchie, E. (1995) *Combating truancy in schools,* David Fulton.

▇▇▇▇ Bullying

Selected readings

Bullying: don't suffer in silence: an anti-bullying pack for schools (1994), Department for Education, London.
Maines, B. & Robinson, G. (1991) *The no blame approach to bullying,* Lame Duck Publishing, Bristol.
Sharp, S. & Smith, P. (1994) *Tackling bullying in your school: a practical handbook for teachers,* Routledge, London.
Skinner, A. (1992) *Bullying: an annotated bibliography of literature and resources,* Youth Work Press/Calouste Gulbenkian Foundation (UK branch), Leicester.
Tattum, D. & Herbert, G. (1990) *Bullying: A positive response,* CIHE Learning Resources Centre, Cardiff.

▇▇▇▇ Behaviour and classroom practices

Selected readings

Allen, B. (1994) *If it makes my life easier to write a policy on behaviour,* Lucky Duck Publishing, Bristol.
Bennett, N. & Dunne, E. (1992) *Managing classroom groups,* Simon & Schuster, Hemel Hempstead.
Creemers, B.P.M. (1994) *The effective classroom,* Cassell, London.
Dunne, R., & Wragg, T. (1994) *Effective teaching,* Routledge, London.
Kyriacou, C. (1989) *Effective teaching in school,* Blackwell, Oxford.
Rogers, B. (1991) *You know the fair rule: strategies for making the hard job of discipline in school easier,* Longman, London.
Wragg, E.C. (1993) *Class management,* Routledge, London.

Useful addresses

National Association for Special Educational Needs, York House, Exhall Grange, Wheelright Lane, Coventry, CV7 9HP, 01203 362414.
This association publishes the following quarterly journals: *Support for Learning, British Journal of Special Education.*

▉ Study skills

Selected readings
Coles, M., White, C. & Brown, P. (1993) *Learning matters: Active approaches to studying,* A resource for teaching about studying, course work, revision and exams, Carel Press, Carlisle.
Devine, T.G. (1987) 2nd edition *Teaching study skills: a guide for teachers,* Allyn and Bacon, Boston, Mass.
McBride, P. (1994) *Study Skills for Success: Practical tips for homework, projects, GCSEs and GNVQs,* Hobsons/CRAC, Cambridge.

▉ Counselling and support

Selected readings
Bovair, K. & McLaughin, C. (Eds) (1993), *Counselling in schools,* David Fulton, London.
Brammer, L.M. (1979) *The helping relationship: process and skills,* Prentice-Hall, Englewood Cliffs.
Crompton, M. (1992), *Children and Counselling,* Edward Arnold, London.
Galloway, D. (1990) *Pupils welfare and counselling: an approach to personal and social education across the curriculum,* Longman, London.
Hamblin, D.H., (1993) *The teacher and counselling,* Simon & Schuster, Hemel Hempstead.
Langham, M. & Parker, V. (1989) *Counselling skills for teachers,* Framework Press, Lancaster.

Useful addresses

British Association of Counselling, 1 Regent Place, Rugby, CV21 2PJ, 01788 578328.
Counselling and Career Development Unit (CCDU), University of Leeds, 44 Clarendon Rd, Leeds, LS2 9PJ 01532 334913, This unit provides in-service training, consultancy, research and evaluation services.

National Association for Pastoral Care in Education (NAPCE), c/o Department of Education, University of Warwick, Coventry, CV4 7AL, 01203 523810. Publishes the *Journal of Pastoral Care in Education*.

▮▮▮▮ Developing links with home and community

Bastiani, J. & Doyle, N. (1994) *Home and School – Building a better partnership,* National Consumer Council.

▮▮▮▮ Children's Rights

Useful addresses

Advisory Centre for Education, 1B Aberdeen Studios, 22 Highbury Grove, London N5 2EA, 0171 354 8321. This centre provides information and advice on all aspects of education.

Childright – A bulletin of law and policy affecting children and young people in England and Wales. Published by The Children's Legal Centre, 20 Compton Terrace, London, N1 2UN, 0171 359 6251.

Young carers

Carers National Association, 20–25 Glasshouse Yard, London EC1A 4JS, 0171 490 8818 (office), 0171 490 8898 (carer's line). This association gives information about and for young carers.

Children of travellers

National Association of Teachers of Travellers, The Graiseley Site, Pool Street, Wolverhampton, WV2 4NE. This association can provide information and resources relating to the education of traveller children.

Index